a gift from

First Aviation Services Inc.

THE GATHERING
OF MUSTANGS & LEGENDS

★ THE FINAL ROUNDUP ★

Editor: Lyn Freeman

Copyeditor: Jamie Ericson

Design Consultant: Creative Spot

Photo Editor: Paul Bowen

Printed and bound in Canada: Friesens

Library of Congress Control Number: 2011939274

ISBN: 978-0-615-53732-0

Stock photography for use in advertising and promotional materials available by written permission only. For availability and pricing, contact: The Gathering Foundation, Inc. (407) 846-7251 or www.gatheringfoundation.org

To purchase a book directly: (407) 846-7251

THE GATHERING
OF MUSTANGS & LEGENDS

 The Final Roundup

Foreword by Lee Lauderback

LEE LAUDERBACK

During four magnificent days in September 2007, a monumental event took place at the former Rickenbacker Air Force Base in Columbus, Ohio. A collection of 77 P-51 Mustangs and 51 Legends joined ranks to celebrate the heritage of this incredible aircraft and many of the people who took it to war.

Legends, such as R. A. "Bob" Hoover, Col. Bud Anderson, Maj. Gen. Donald Strait, Betty Blake, and many more were there to once again be close to this terrific fighter and help make history. Designers, builders, crew chiefs, WASPs, and Tuskegee Airmen, along with many other pilots and aces, wandered the flight line sharing their stories and experiences of taking the P-51 into combat. They watched once again as the Mustang took to the skies, this time not going off to combat, but rather flying as a tribute to them.

Like the Mustang, the United States Air Force is rich with history and tradition. With their support, the Gathering of Mustangs and Legends event also celebrated that heritage with the first ever USAF Heritage Week through an incredible display of Air Force airpower. There were tactical flight demonstrations by the F-16 Viper, the F-15 Eagle, and the F-22 Raptor. Additionally, twice each day the Mustang flew in close formation with today's fighters in the Heritage Flight Program, a extraordinary contrast of just how far modern fighter technology has come in the past 65 years.

The Gathering of Mustangs and Legends was the quintessential event, a first class airshow, a special collection of man and machine. I would like to personally thank the owners and operators of these magnificent Mustangs that made this event so special. Without their passion for and investment in preservation, the Mustang would not be flying today. These special people allowed the Mustang to be there in force and once again dominate the skies. I would also like to thank the people in attendance who came from all parts of the world to pay tribute to the men and women who helped make the P-51 so legendary.

For those of you who could not make the event, this book will allow you to share the excitement through the tremendous photographs of the talented "Shooters" we had on board. Photographers such as Paul Bowen, who led our photo team, captured this historical gathering, and it is through them that we can relive this event for years to come.

I would also like to thank Angela West who shared my dream and worked for three years to make this event a success. And to the sponsors, especially Jim Hagedorn of The Scotts Miracle-Gro

Company, a former F-16 fighter pilot and current Mustang owner and pilot, who shared our vision. Additionally, I would like to personally thank the Columbus Regional Airport Authority who allowed us to use their historic airport for the event. And finally, to all the volunteers, especially my Flight Operations Team, Maj. Gen. Dave Robinson who put the "51 Flight" together, Col. Brian Bishop who commanded the Ops Desk, and Maj. Kerry "Tids" Tidmore who ran the daily schedule and solved most problems. All took their valuable time to help not only make the event exciting but safe.

"P-51 Mustang," a simple name that says so much. Seldom in history has there been a machine born of war that has made such a broad impact on history and so many lives. From its first days of combat over the skies of Europe to peaceful flights over today's countryside, the Mustang has had a long and distinguished history. Share now a special moment in time, a gathering of man and machine, both legend and legendary.

Mustangs Forever,
Lee Lauderback

MUSTANG LEGACY

In 1940, the United States' armed forces were not among the top ten most formidable in the world. When President Franklin D. Roosevelt told the nation he wanted the United States to build 50,000 airplanes, people snickered at such baseless optimism. But the reality is we did make that many airplanes. From January 1, 1940 until V-J Day on August 14, 1945, America produced more than 300,000 military aircraft for the U.S. military and its allies. In just the month of March 1944, more than 9,000 aircraft came off the assembly lines. At the pinnacle of that production came the North American P-51 Mustang. This book is a loving and lasting tribute to that remarkable airplane and the men and women who made it the most recognized and admired combat fighter of all time.

Photo: Courtesy John Dibbs Collection

THE LEGACY BEGINS

Few would disagree that the North American P-51 Mustang is the most iconic fighter aircraft in the world. More than 15,500 were built, and approximately 8,000 were P-51Ds. Mustangs flew 213,873 sorties during World War II, more than any other fighter. The P-51 shot down 4,950 enemy planes, more than any other Allied aircraft.

P-51s are even credited with chasing down the first jet fighters, the Messerschmitt 262 (ME-262), as well as German V-1 rockets launched toward London. Today only about 160 airworthy North American P-51 Mustangs survive.

Photo: Courtesy of Jack Cook

The top Air Force Mustang ace was George Preddy, who shot down 26.83 planes, 23.83 scored with the P-51. He was shot down and killed by friendly fire on Christmas Day, 1944.

Ultimately the North American P-51 Mustang shifted the entire war effort and is said to have caused Reichsmarschall Herman Göring, commander of the German Luftwaffe, to say, "When I saw Mustangs over Berlin, I knew the jig was up."

Despite the advent of the jet fighter, the P-51 Mustang continued in military roles for the next 40 years, with the last Mustang retired by the Dominican Air Force in 1984.

Photo: Courtesy John Dibbs Collection

MUSTANGS IN COMBAT

Photo: Courtesy of Jack Cook

The Royal Air Force's (RAF) Mk I was the first version of the Mustang to be used in combat. The mission profile was both aerial reconnaissance and ground attack. Later the RAF began using the Mustang as an aerial escort for naval ships and low-altitude interception of enemy aircraft.

The Mustang proved a formidable adversary to Luftwaffe pilots flying the Focke-Wulf 190 (FW-190), which had proven to out perform the RAF Spitfire and increased Allied aircrew losses.

The first American variants of the Mustang to see combat were the A-36 Invader and P-51A Apache during the China-Burma-India Theatre. This was the same campaign made famous by General Claire Chennault and his famous "Flying Tigers." It was during this time that the USAAF realized the potential of this new fighter.

Before the introduction of the Mustang in the air war over Europe, Allied fighters did not have the range to escort bombers all the way to their target and back. That left the big bombers vulnerable to Luftwaffe fighter attack. But with the Mustang's extended range capabilities, the P-51 could cover the bombers for the entire mission. That single fact was enough to change the face of the war.

The first production Merlin-powered P-51Bs were assigned to the 354th "Pioneer Mustang Group" in December 1943. Flying escort missions for the 8th Air Force's B-17s and B-24s, the P-51B had the range to provide protection for bomber crews deep into Nazi Germany.

Combat statistics proved the Mustang to be a superior fighter. By early 1944, the P-51 was credited with an average of 13 kills per 100 sorties. This was three times the kill rate of the P-47 and P-38. The Mustangs also enjoyed a kill to loss ratio of nearly 5:1.

By the middle of 1944 the P-51D Mustang began operational service with the likes of the 352nd Fighter Group "Blue Nose Bastards of Bodney," 4th Fighter Group "Debden Eagles," and many other operational units throughout Europe and the Pacific. The D Model had increased visibility due to the bubble canopy and increased armament and range.

After World War II, the Mustang went on to see combat in Korea and in later years participated in many "guerrilla" wars that took place in South America.

The P-51 Mustang was designed in 1940 as North American Aviation's solution to the significant losses Allied air forces were sustaining over the skies of Europe during World War II. When paired with the Rolls-Royce-designed Merlin engine, the Mustang gained the range and performance that allowed it to escort and protect Allied bomber forces deep into enemy territory.

Mustang Facts:

Max Speed	505 MPH
Combat Radius	325 miles with initial tanks 750 miles with two 130-gallon tanks
Weights	7,125 lbs. empty 12,300 lbs. combat ready
Service Ceiling	41,900 feet
Armament	6 x .50 caliber machine guns 400 rounds each inboard 270 rounds each center and outboard
Dimensions	Span: 37 feet, 1/2 inch Length: 32 feet, 3 inches Height: 12 feet, 2 inches

Mustang Pilot Aces: 281

Number of Mustangs Produced: 15,686

Number of Airworthy Mustangs Remaining Today: 160+

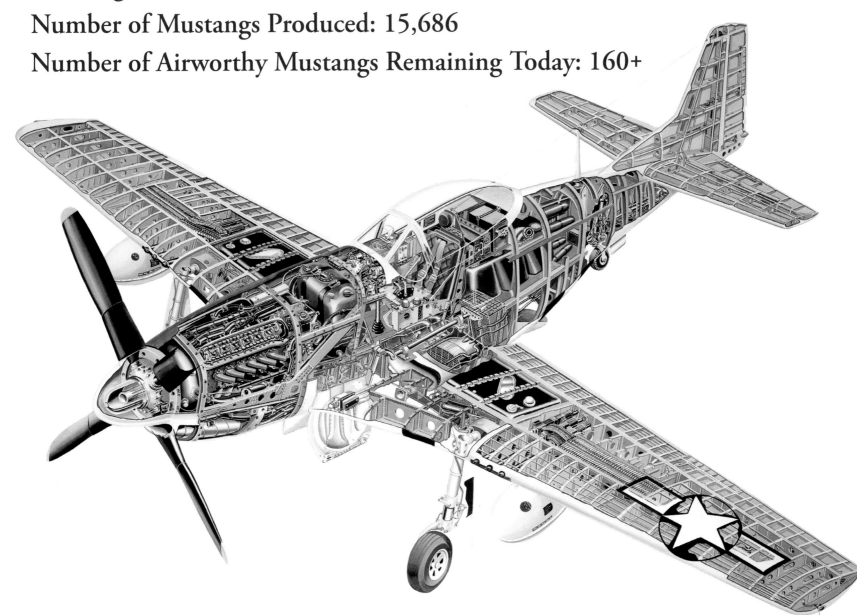

Illustration by John Batchelor

DESIGN

Photo: Courtesy Stan Piet

When the new combination astonished pilots at nearly any altitude, they knew they had a truly advanced fighter.

Born from a company that had never before designed a fighter aircraft, North American Aviation (NAA) created the Mustang — from slide rule to prototype aircraft — in an unprecedented 120 days.

The Royal Air Force (RAF) was in negotiations with NAA as a potential supplier for the Curtiss-designed P-40 when J. H. "Dutch" Kindelberger, company president, convinced the British that North American Aviation had the capability to build a totally new and technologically advanced fighter to suit their requirements.

Then Sir Henry Self, on behalf of the British Purchasing Commission, agreed to NAA's proposal with the stipulation that they could deliver a prototype in just 120 days. North American met this expectation and the maiden flight of the NA-73X took place on October 26, 1940.

From the start, the Mustang design incorporated many new and innovative features. Aerodynamic advances such as a streamlined fuselage, NACA laminar flow wing, sealed ailerons, and airflow ducting all contributed to the Mustang's excellent performance and handling qualities.

And, while initial flights revealed some minor engine overheating problems, it didn't take long to prove that the NA-73X was more than capable; it represented a major breakthrough in fighter design that would eventually turn the tide of the air war in Europe.

In fact, the RAF ordered 320 aircraft before the first prototype even took flight. Under the terms of the contract, two of the new fighters were sent to the Army Air Corps for testing. This American version was designated the XP-51. While the aircraft's performance raised eyebrows, the United States Army Air Force (USAAF) was still focused on the mass production of the P-38 Lighting and P-47 Thunderbolt.

The British determined their new Allison-powered fighter excelled at lower altitudes; however, performance significantly degraded above 17,000 feet. As a solution, the British modified the Mustang with the Rolls-Royce Merlin 61 engine. This engine with its two-stage super-charger gave the aircraft astonishing performance at nearly any altitude.

The joining of the Merlin to the Mustang led to arguably the most successful fighter aircraft of all time.

The Rolls-Royce and Packard Merlin Engine

Considered one of the best engines to be widely produced during World War II, the Rolls-Royce Merlin engine was without a doubt one of the most successfully employed aircraft engines in history. During World War II, the Merlin could be found on any number of different types of Allied aircraft, but it was when the engine was introduced to the P-51 Mustang that it changed the face of the war.

The Merlin is a 12-cylinder, 60° "V," 27-liter, liquid cooled piston aircraft engine capable of mustering 1,700 horsepower (HP). The first Merlin was built in 1936 by Rolls-Royce to fill the 700 and 1,500 HP gap in their aero engine line. The first Merlin only saw a production run of 172 before the adoption of the Merlin II. Ultimately, 19 different types of aircraft were outfitted with Merlin engines, including the Spitfire, Hurricane, P-51, Mosquito, Lancaster, and the P-40F with power outputs ranging from 1,000 HP to over 2,000 HP in the Merlin 66.

In 1940, an agreement was reached between the Packard Company and Rolls-Royce allowing Packard to produce Merlin engines. These American-built engines were produced by an assembly line, rather than the Europeans' method of meticulously hand building each engine. Surprisingly enough, American engines actually improved the maintainability of the engine by allowing easier use of interchangeable parts.

Because of the Merlin's dynamic two-speed, two-stage (in later models) engine driven supercharger, it was capable of delivering high power at altitudes in excess of 30,000 feet. This made the engine the ideal choice for the North American P-51. The first of the Mustangs, the P-51As, were outfitted with Allison

V-1710 engines. These engines, due to GE's inability to produce a sufficient quantity, lacked the turbochargers that would enable the P-51 to have suitable high altitude performance. The P-51A was forced to stay relatively low because of this (+/- 20,000 feet) and was not able to fly escort for the Allies' high altitude bombers. In 1943, the next model of the Mustang took to the skies with a Packard Merlin V-1650 and outperformed the Allison-powered P-51A in all aspects. The rate of climb doubled at all altitudes, and the P-51B's level flight speed at 29,800 feet was 441 mph, a full 100 mph faster than the P-51A at that altitude.

The Mustang went on to strike fear into the heart of the Axis powers with its newfound ability to fight just as well up high as it could down low. According to the pilots who flew them, the new Merlin-powered Mustangs were some of the most honest and well-performing aircraft they had ever flown. These P-51s were also some of the only piston-powered airplanes that would ever shoot down enemy jets. When the Germans introduced their jet fighter, the ME-262, it was the P-51 Mustang with a Merlin under the hood that led to many Axis losses and ultimately secured the Allied victory.

MODELS

Photo: Courtesy of Jack Cook

P-51A Apache

The Army first saw delivery of the P-51A Apache in March of 1943. This Mustang was powered by an Allison V-1710-81 engine that incorporated a simple supercharger, which, unfortunately, did not have the capability to produce adequate horsepower for combat much above 20,000 feet. Capable of 390 mph at 20,000 feet, the P-51A was one of the best fighters in the United States Army Air Force (USAAF) inventory below 22,000 feet (according to the AAF School of Applied Tactics). The armament consisted of four .30 caliber machine guns and up to two 500-pound bombs. Recognizable mostly by its Aero-Products three-blade, 10' 6" propeller, and birdcage canopy, very few remain today of the 310 originally produced.

Photo: Courtesy of Jack Cook

A-36 Invader

The A-36 was the ground attack variant of the P-51A. First deployed by the United States in the Mediterranean Theater in 1943, it was utilized with mild success. This early Mustang was powered by the Allison V-1710 and featured hydraulic dive brakes on each wing to make the aircraft a more stable dive bomber. Its top speed was 358 mph at 5,000 feet, slower than the P-51A mostly due to added weight. A-36s incorporated the use of six .50 caliber machine guns, four in the wings and two actually located in the nose. It also had the capability to carry two 500-pound bombs. These ground attack Mustangs proved to be great fighters at low altitude, scoring a total of 101 aerial victories in World War II. However, a total of 177 were lost in action, mostly because of enemy ground fire and the associated hazards with low altitude and strafing operations.

Photo: Courtesy of Jack Cook

P-51B Mustang

The P-51B was the first American Mustang to be introduced with the famous Merlin V-1650, which produced almost 500 more horsepower than the older Allison engine. This is where the Mustang gets all its glory, as the Packard-built Rolls-Royce Merlin engine utilized a two-speed supercharger (later two stage) allowing sea level engine performance up to altitudes as high as 35,000 feet. First flying in May 1943, the P-51Bs were manufactured at North American Aviation's Inglewood plant in California. These aircraft are recognizable by the addition of a four-bladed Hamilton-Standard propeller, a birdcage style canopy that offered little in the way of rearward visibility, and four .50 caliber machine guns (two in each wing). With external fuel, these Mustangs could fly almost 2,000 miles nonstop, making them capable of escorting Allied high altitude bombers all the way to and from their targets.

Photo: Courtesy of Jack Cook

P-51C Mustang

P-51Cs were identical to the B models, the only difference being where the aircraft were produced. While the P-51Bs were manufactured in California, demand for the aircraft reached numbers impossible for one plant to produce, so additional Mustangs were built at North American's Dallas, Texas plant. The aircraft produced from the Dallas plant received the C designation not for a different aircraft version, but for a different production facility. The B/C models were able to achieve a maximum level flight speed of 439 mph at 25,000 feet, with a service ceiling as high as 42,000 feet. A total of 1,750 P-51Cs rolled out of North American's Dallas facility.

P-51D Mustang

Photo: Courtesy of Brad Lauderback

Considered the definitive Mustang, the P-51D featured several modifications and improvements over the B/C models, most notably the teardrop bubble canopy. This new canopy greatly improved all-around visibility, and with the removal of the decking behind the cockpit, the pilot could now look directly to the rear. Other improvements included a reworked wing that would accommodate six .50 caliber machine guns, and improved arrangement of the ammo chutes resolved many of the gun-jamming problems. The ailerons on the P-51D were improved by adding a seal to the leading edge, thus relieving some of the stick pressure required when maneuvering. Approximately 8,000 P-51Ds rolled off the North American line, and the first of them saw action in 1944 – right in time for the D-Day invasion.

P-51H Mustang

Photo: Courtesy of Jack Cook

Developed as a light-weight Mustang, the H model was designed to be the best performing of all the North American Mustang variants. This P-51 was completely redesigned to weigh in a full 600 pounds less than the P-51D. In fact, there were not any interchangeable parts between the H and D/K models, and the V-1650-9 was chosen to power the P-51H. When called upon, a water/alcohol injection gave the airplane a war emergency horsepower (WEP) rating of 2,200 HP above 10,000 feet. Other modifications of the H included longer fuselage length, a taller tail, a redesigned canopy, removable ammo boxes, AeroProducts 11-foot unimatic propeller, and a decreased center fuselage tank capacity (55 gallons) for better stability – just to name a few. It was by far the fastest Mustang, topping out at 487 mph at 25,000 feet. While P-51Hs entered service before V-J Day, none saw any combat. Most of the 555 H models produced ended up going on to National Guard units throughout the country after the war.

P-51K Mustang

Photo: Courtesy of Don Schoen

Almost identical to the P-51D, the main difference between the two aircraft is the propeller. The P-51D utilized the Hamilton Standard propeller. Unfortunately, that company could not meet the demand for the number of Mustangs being produced by North American at the Dallas plant. Therefore, the decision was made to supply AeroProducts' propellers to keep Mustang production going. These props were hollow and often not balanced well, but they worked. Many Ks were field-modified with the Hamilton-Standard propeller. Approximately 1,500 P-51Ks were built, all at the Dallas, Texas North American facility.

Photo: Courtesy of Jack Cook

P/F-82 Twin Mustang

The P/F-82 was the last propeller-driven fighter acquired in quantity by the USAAF. North American produced 250 of the double-fuselaged Mustangs. It appears to be two Mustang fuselages on one wing, but in reality it was a totally new design. Its purpose was to provide a fighter that could carry a pilot and co-pilot to reduce fatigue on long-range bomber escort missions. Delivery did not begin until early 1946, too late for World War II. Most F-82s were produced as all-weather night fighters, with the first being the F-82F. This version was equipped with the AN/APG-28 tracking radar. These were followed by the F-82G, which carried the SCR-720C search radar. During the Korean Conflict, Japan-based F-82s were among the first USAAF aircraft to operate over Korea. The Twin Mustang also left its mark on aviation history in 1946 when a specially modified P-82 named *Betty Jo* established a non-stop distance record by flying from Hickam Field, Hawaii to Mitchel Field, New York. This record still stands today as the greatest distance flown by an un-refueled fighter.

Photo: Courtesy of Randy Haskin

Cavalier Mustang

Cavalier Aircraft Corp. was founded in 1957 by Sarasota, Florida newspaper publisher David Lindsay. Cavalier's objective was to construct a high-speed executive transport from surplus military Mustangs. Each aircraft rolled off the Cavalier production line with modern avionics, plush interiors, a luggage bay, and sporty civilian paint schemes. Various models were produced mostly differing in internal fuel capacity. The most notable version was the Cavalier 2000, which incorporated 96-gallon tip tanks and a 14-inch height addition to the vertical stabilizer. In addition to the civil market, Cavalier also overhauled and upgraded Mustangs for military use by various third world countries throughout the 1960s.

Photo: Courtesy of Randy Haskin

TEMCO TF-51 Mustang

Under contract from North American Aviation, Texas Engineering and Manufacturing Corporation (TEMCO) took 15 Dallas-built P-51Ds off the North American Aviation production line and converted them to full dual cockpit/dual control trainers. To accommodate the rear cockpit, the 85-gallon fuselage fuel tank was removed and the battery and radio equipment were shifted. Additionally, an elongated canopy was fitted to give the rear seat occupant more headroom. Once off the TEMCO production line, these aircraft were mainly allocated to Air National Guard Units as the mainstream United States Air Force was quickly moving into the jet age. In addition to these 15 aircraft, Cavalier built eight TF-51s from either parts purchased from TEMCO or produced from TEMCO specs.

RESTORATION

Preserving the legacy of the Mustang is not an easy task. Of the thousands of P-51s built, there are approximately 160 left that are airworthy. Those that have survived through decades of neglect have found rebirth at the hands of skilled mechanics that not only restore them to the sky but restore the history that they have guarded within.

More than mechanics, the men and women who bring these magnificent examples of the period's aviation know-how back to life are more akin to museum conservators, following the most intricate details and drawings to restore the aircraft to new condition.

North American Aviation created cutting edge technology and a beautiful work of art in the Mustang. They then had the ability to mass-produce it and all its many specialty parts and components thousands of times to perfection.

Beyond the technology was heart. The hundreds of thousands of workers who made the warbirds of World War II made them with extreme care. These planes were not being made for nameless pilots but for their sons, fathers, brothers, and husbands. That care and skill is the reason many have survived to fly again.

Restoration is only the beginning of what is needed to maintain a Mustang. To keep them flying takes vigilance and craftsmanship, skills that are becoming as rare as the planes themselves.

No matter how many rivets are replaced, engines rebuilt, frames re-skinned, or paint applied, the heart, soul, and history of these planes still exist waiting to share stories with the next person who hears it roar overhead one more time.

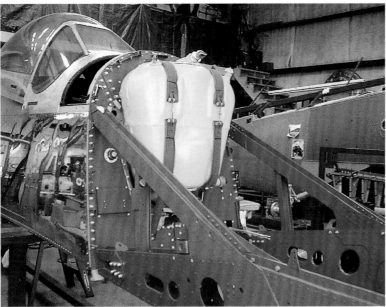

Mustang restoration is nothing short of an art form. Components such as wings, fuselages, and Merlin engines can come from a surprising number of places. The unique knowledge to get all of these things to come together is what keeps the P-51 Mustang flying today.

THE 1999 GATHERING

In April 1999, 65 P-51 Mustangs and 12 Mustang Legends from WWII came to Stallion 51 Corporation in Kissimmee, Florida for a class reunion of sorts; the Class of 51, reuniting the planes and the pilots who made history.

Aircraft and pilots from all over the country flew to Stallion 51 to participate in a two-day seminar on flying the Mustang safely, which included recurrent training, maintenance, and, of course, formation flying. The pilots may have come to learn, but the Mustangs came to play. Because, where else could a Mustang find another Mustang to play with?

Hungry for History

As the Mustangs flew in they brought with them a following of fans hungry for history. Thousands of people showed up every day, hanging out on the ramp just to watch and listen – to hear the Merlins start up as they went out for a training flight, to watch a pilot go through the pre-flight walk around, to catch a glimpse of the aces they had only read about or seen in black and white. Everyone who was there that weekend witnessed something special, not an airshow in the traditional sense, but a communion of sorts honoring the sacrifices of talented men and women who designed, maintained, and flew these great machines. They remembered times when we as a nation were called upon to do great things and we answered as loudly as a Merlin engine at takeoff.

Because of the somewhat surprising attendance to the original Gathering in 1999, the decision was made to do it again – one last time.

As the Mustangs lined up for a training sortie, thousands of attendees lined the taxiway like a celebrity red carpet. They waited patiently to watch the pilots climb onto the wing and slip into the cockpit, to hear the Merlins start up, to smell the first puff of exhaust as they kicked over, to watch the Mustangs do the "tail wheel tango" as they wiggled to the runway and took off in formation to play in the clouds.

While the pilots were airborne working on their formation skills with the other Mustangs, the Legends gathered to share stories with the crowd and each other. They were gracious with their time, answering questions, signing autographs, and taking pictures with their admirers. They were the rock stars, but they were humbled by all the attention. Some of the pilots were famous and others almost nameless to the thousands who gathered, but all of them had stories to tell of their time flying the greatest fighter ever built.

Crowds gathered around Bud Anderson and his wingmen recounting the days when they flew together. They could feel the

magnetism of Robin Olds, sensing why men followed him into battle in both WWII and Vietnam. They heard Lee Archer's stories of fighting the enemy over the front lines as well as prejudice on the home front. The Legends spoke to a crowd hungry for every word, telling stories of friendship and fellowship and remembering friends that could not make the gathering. The interactions were priceless – history told by those who made it. Eager listeners relived the tales as they clung to the fence watching the planes come and go.

For those who attended the 1999 Gathering of Mustangs and Legends, they knew they had been a part of something special, a "Warbird Woodstock." Their taste of living history left them wanting more – more flying, more stories, more time with the Legends before they were gone forever. **The Gathering of Mustangs and Legends of 1999 ignited the passion for another gathering of the greatest generation of planes and pilots, and so we rounded everyone up one last time at The Gathering of Mustangs and Legends 2007, The Final Roundup.**

THE 2007 GATHERING

77 P-51s waited on the ramp, the largest number of Mustangs to come together since World War II. 51 Legends, the men and women who flew and supported the Mustang, had come from across America. World-class airshow performers prepared to showcase stunts and demonstrations. And because this aviation event was held on the 60th anniversary of the United States Air Force, a showcase of military airpower, including the USAF Thunderbirds and modern fighters participating in the Heritage Flight Program, joined the celebration.

The result? Over four days more than 150,000 people came to see this once in a lifetime event.

THE HISTORY OF RICKENBACKER

It is difficult to imagine a more fitting venue for The Gathering of Mustangs and Legends than Rickenbacker International Airport. Its rich military history has so touched – and been touched by – the Mustang. The airport debuted in 1942 as the Mustang was first entering combat in Europe. Christened as Lockbourne Army Air Base, its mission was quickly converted from training glider pilots to training B-17 bomber crews, many of whom ultimately owed their lives to their "little friend" the P-51. Immediately after the war, Lockbourne Air Force Base became home to the famed Tuskegee Airmen, whose legendary success protecting Allied bombers from German fighters made them and their red tail P-51s the escorts of choice. The 55th Fighter Wing and its Mustangs also called Lockbourne home after the war. In 1974, the base was renamed Rickenbacker Air Force Base, after World War I "ace of aces" and Columbus native Eddie Rickenbacker. Today a public airport, Rickenbacker continues to play an important part in our nation's defense as home to the Ohio Air

National Guard's 121st Aerial Refueling Wing, which has served around the world in both peacetime and combat roles. With The Gathering of Mustangs and Legends bringing so many aircraft, Legends, Tuskegee Airmen, and other veterans together in a place that had touched so many of them, this once in a lifetime event has added yet another page to Rickenbacker Airport's rich and storied history.

Many fighter groups, including The Tuskegee Airmen, used The Gathering as an opportunity to unite with old and new friends.

As the sun rose on the ramp at Rickenbacker International, the years of preparation for The Gathering of Mustangs and Legends were about to become worthwhile. Rows and rows of warbirds were standing at silent attention. Civilian performers were on hand. The media were preparing lights and cameras. Everyone there sensed what a truly special event was about to unfold.

Inclement weather in areas across the United States and in Columbus made it challenging for some of the aircraft to arrive. Additionally, several of the scheduled warbirds had mechanical issues that grounded them before they could even get airborne. Nevertheless, the Mustang community came. In droves. By the morning of the first day of the event, 77 Mustangs stretched wingtip to wingtip across the ramp.

Outside the gates at Rickenbacker International Airport, long lines for admission had formed hours before the event would begin. There were moms and dads, kids with toy airplanes, adults born long after World War II, as well as veterans of nearly every recent conflict. Among them all was a sense that what they were about to see would be something they would remember for the rest of their lives.

For four days, the ground and air over Columbus, Ohio traveled back more than sixty years to the 1940s, arguably the most remarkable years in the comparatively short history of aviation when more men and machines were mobilized than any time in modern history.

FIRST LOOK

Walking through the gates and onto the tarmac was nothing short of time travel. The airport had been transformed into a World War II airfield. Two P-38s sat side by side, and here was a P-47 Thunderbolt, and over there a P-40 Warhawk and a P-63 Kingcobra. But mostly it was the Mustangs – 77 of them, more than had been assembled in one place for more than 60 years.

The opening ceremony was a world class event on its own. As the giant American flag unfurled from the skydiver's leg and the National Anthem played, the field became motionless as more than a hundred thousand people stood in reverence and respect for their country and all that she's accomplished. Attending Legend Bill Creech said, "The opening...that was absolutely eye watering. I'll simply never get too old to not be madly in love with our Old Glory. To see her floating down following a jumper, in all her glory, is a sight I'll NEVER, NEVER tire of."

Concerns about attracting the interest of younger generations disappeared. There seemed to be a natural affinity between kids and the amazing P-51 Mustang.

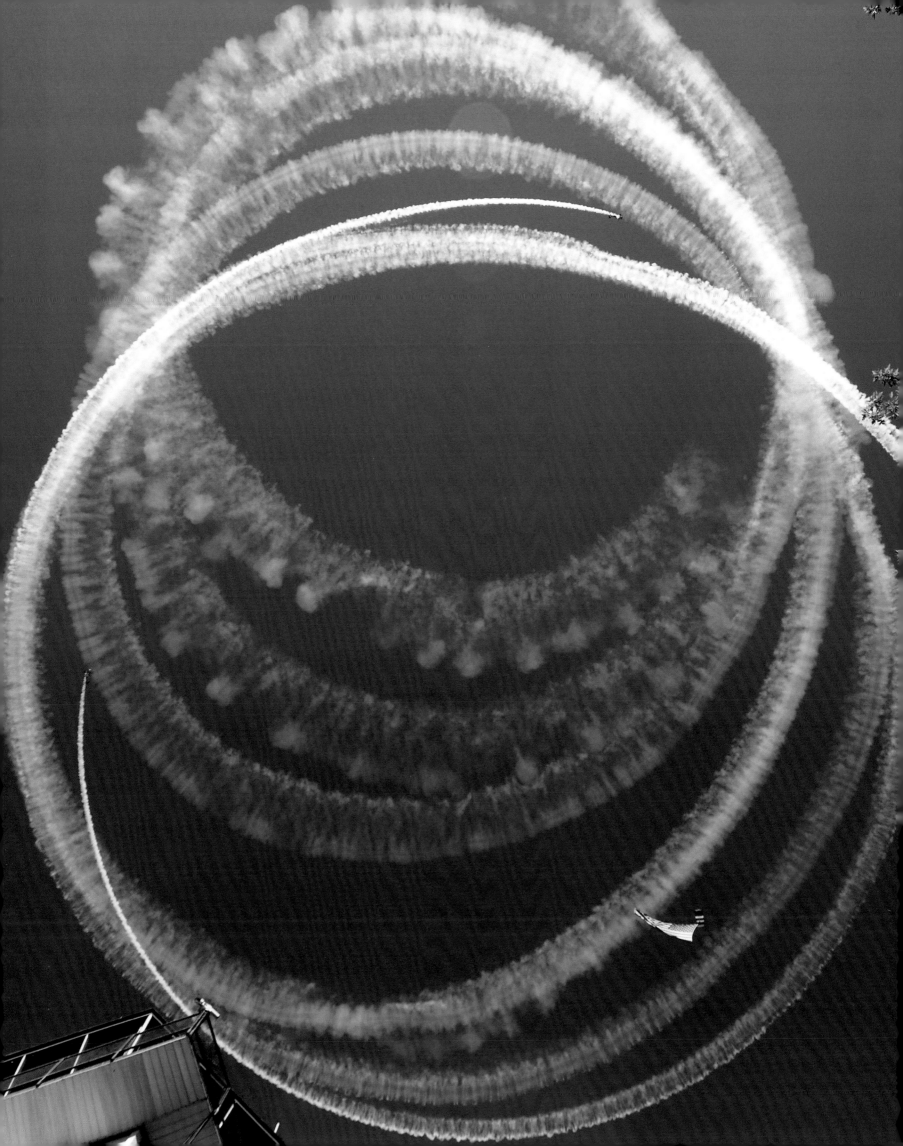

Formations of Mustangs rendezvoused with bombers on a daily basis at The Gathering as they flew for the eager crowd.

Attendees had the ability to walk right up and touch the Mustangs, a remarkable experience for many. Often they were greeted by aircraft owners or war vets who were happy to explain the features of the aircraft and supervise a customized tour of the warbird.

The Gathering of Mustangs and Legends was accented by authentic uniforms and aviation paraphernalia from the War.

Fighter pilots of the future, United States Air Force Academy cadets pose on the wing of a Mustang.

HUNDREDS OF THOUSANDS

More than 150,000 visitors from over 26 countries came to see the greatest overall collection of World War II aircraft anywhere in the world. In addition to the fighters, there were two B-25 Mitchell bombers, a B-17 Flying Fortress, and a four-engine British Avro Lancaster bomber. The waves of guests surrounded the aircraft in such numbers that the warbirds were often indiscernible from the sea of people who were there to admire them.

Formidable aircraft soon disappeared into a sea of more than 150,000 eager onlookers. While the weather was inclement at the start of the event, blue skies and sunshine arrived by show time and remained on duty for all four days.

Being able to get close to the Mustangs was no accident. Hundreds of thousands of people got closer to the warbirds than they'd ever been, and many even got to try the warbird on for size by waiting in line for a personal moment in the cockpit (facing page).

AIRSHOW PERFORMERS

The ten to twelve million people who attend each year make airshows the largest outdoor professional sporting events in North America, larger than baseball, larger than football. Long lines at the gate hours before the show opened meant that the 150,000+ who had come to Columbus, Ohio from all over the world knew The Gathering of Mustangs and Legends was going to be something very special, creating memories for a lifetime.

USAF THUNDERBIRDS

Leonardo da Vinci said, "For once you have tasted flight you will walk the earth with your eyes turned skywards, for there you have been and there you will long to return." No words better describe the soul of the aviators and enthusiasts who assembled at the 2007 Gathering of Mustangs and Legends.

As a six-year-old girl flying in a KC-135, I tasted flight and from that moment on had my eyes turned skywards. Being a member of the USAF Thunderbirds was an honor and a privilege, but being a part of the Gathering was a once in a lifetime opportunity. The GML brought together the dreams, determination, and destiny of people, planes, and location. For me, this weekend intertwined the past with the present in order to preserve aviation history for the future. Nothing showcased this more than the vintage P-51, the WWII workhorse of the Army Air Corps, and the F-16, the fighter workhorse of today's Air Force. The men and women who flew the P-51 also represent the evolution of aviation: from WASPs like Betty Blake, to Tuskegee Airmen like Roscoe Brown and Lee Archer (also an ace), to WWII aces like Arthur Jeffrey and Merle Olmstead.

This event brought the past and present together culminating the Air Force's first-ever Air Force Heritage Week at Rickenbacker Airport. Witnessing the P-51 sharing the sky with the F-22 is a memory ingrained in my mind. For me, however, the location was as much a part of the week as the planes and people. My first assignment was the 94th Fighter Squadron and home to Eddie Rickenbacker and the historical "Hat-in-the-Ring" gang.

The Gathering of Mustangs and Legends showcased heroes of yesterday leading the way for aviation today and made a connection for me to the aviators who defended our freedoms in WWI and WWII, reigniting my pride of serving in the Air Force today. This book helps preserve a monumental weekend of flight for future generations to reflect and understand the greatest generation and their impact on the world as we know it today.

- Major Samantha Weeks, USAF Thunderbirds #6 - Opposing Solo

The USAF Thunderbirds fly with their traditional paint scheme on the bottom of their F-16 Fighting Falcons. The group has been demonstrating precision flying skills since 1953.

The pursuit of perfection is an overriding theme with the USAF Thunderbirds, even when parking their aircraft.

The United States Air Force was created in 1947 and it was not long afterward that this new branch of the military would want to create a flight demonstration team. The Thunderbirds became the mark of the USAF's best pilots, and the squadron tours the country and much of the world performing aerobatic formation and solo flying, currently in the Lockheed Martin F-16 Fighting Falcon.

The Thunderbirds have honed their skills to the point where pilots can safely fly their aircraft only inches apart.

USAF HERITAGE FLIGHT PROGRAM

Remarkably, The Gathering of Mustangs and Legends coincided with the United States Air Force's (USAF) 60th Anniversary and was elected as the only aviation event named "Air Force Heritage Week." The USAF Heritage Flight Program has been in place for over ten years and is showcased all over the world at various airshows. A Heritage Flight consists of a current USAF fighter flown by an air combat command demonstration team pilot with a historical warbird flown by a trained and certified civilian Heritage Flight pilot. The Heritage Flight formations of modern fighters flying with World War II, Korean, and Vietnam-era fighters, such as the P-51 Mustang and F-86 Sabre, dramatically display the history of USAF air power and proudly support our Air Force's recruiting and retention efforts.

The P-51 Mustang flies lead with the state-of-the-art F-22 Raptor in the classic 2-ship Heritage Flight (above left). The F-22 Raptor is flying slot position with three Mustangs in lead in the 4-ship Heritage Flight (above right). Once more the P-51 flying in the 2-ship classic Heritage Flight but with the F-15 Eagle (above).

Quick Facts

First Flight	September 7, 1997
Number Built	187 (planned)
Crew	1
Engine/Thrust	2 × Pratt & Whitney F119PW-100 Pitch Thrust Vectoring turbofans/35,000+ each
Max Speed	Mach 2.25
Rate of Climb	Classified
Service Ceiling	65,000 Feet

F-22 RAPTOR

2007 was a magical year for the F-22 Demo Team. Not only did we unveil the tactical demonstration of the finest fighter aircraft ever built, but we also had the opportunity to participate in what I consider to be the capstone aviation event of the decade… The Gathering of Mustangs and Legends. From day one of our inaugural season there was no doubt that GML was our number one priority show, and it ended up being one of the most memorable experiences of my military career. Flying the first Raptor demo (which in so many ways is the 21st century equivalent of the P-51) in front of the likes of Bob Hoover, Bud Anderson, Lee Archer, Roscoe Brown, and so many other Legends was nothing shy of remarkable – not to mention nerve-wracking! To them, I was a sierra-hotel young fighter jock that had one of the best rides on the planet. To me, those guys are heroes that I couldn't match on my best day.

- Major Paul "Max" Moga, F-22 demo pilot

F-16 FALCON

Each year as the USAF single ship demonstration schedules begin to form, there is a feeling of anticipation, anticipation for the upcoming show year and a desire to land a few of the really good shows. The Gathering of Mustangs and Legends was a top show listed on the Viper East dream sheet for the 2007 show year. The entire team was elated when we received word that we would be a part of this historic event.

Watching the single Mustang demonstrations, the Horsemen, and the final Flight of the Mustang forces a pilot to think back to a different era in aviation. One where the pilot and machine were one. A time where the aircraft talked to the pilot in flight, and the pilot responded with grace and finesse to get the most out of his fighting machine. Flying was a skill and an art form, each pilot an artist and combat aviator. My F-16 demonstration simply filled a gap from the Mustang to the present.

- Major Jason "Buzzer" Koltes, F-16 demo pilot

The Lockheed Martin F-16 Fighting Falcon (later nicknamed the "Viper") has been a mainstay of U.S. operational readiness for more than three decades. Its relaxed static stability/fly-by-wire gives it a remarkable control input response.

Quick Facts

First Flight	February 2, 1974
Number Built	4,450+
Crew	1
Engine/Thrust	1 x F110-GE-100 afterburning turbofan/28,600 lbf
Max Speed	Mach 2+
Rate of Climb	50,000 ft/min
Service Ceiling	60,000+ feet

F-15 EAGLE

For me, airshow flying was all about the relationships. I was extremely privileged to be part of such a small community, a fraternity of aviators who shared a common passion...flying. To be selected to perform at such a historic event was very humbling. Knowing that I had the opportunity to meet and perform for an audience of true legends was something that I will never forget.

Since I was a kid, the P-51 has been a symbol of air power, and to be able to fly wing tip to wing tip with one of the greatest aircraft ever made was incredibly special. But meeting and interacting with the pilots that have flown such magnificent aircraft made it even more so. Aviation is all about experiences, and Mustang drivers represent one of the brightest lights of American aviation. I was honored to spend the weekend amongst these great machines and amazing people.

- Captain William "Baron" Bierenkoven, F-15 demo pilot

The F-15 Eagle is considered to be among the most successful modern fighters with over 100 aerial combat victories and no losses in dogfights. The F-15 is planned to remain operational until at least 2025.

Quick Facts

First Flight	July 27, 1972
Number Built	1,198
Crew	1
Engine/Thrust	2 × Pratt & Whitney F100 or -220 afterburning turbofans/25,000lbf
Max Speed	Mach 2.5
Rate of Climb	50,000 ft/min
Service Ceiling	65,000+ feet

AEROSHELL AEROBATIC TEAM

Our team was honored when we were chosen to perform. When we arrived, it was obvious that this event was different than any we had flown before. To have all those Mustangs and the WWII pilots and crews there was very humbling because we fly these warbirds for the pure joy of flying pieces of history. These pilots and their crews were flying Mustangs because they were defending a nation. Each time the pilots took the Mustangs into combat there was a chance they were not coming back. Because of the sacrifices that these brave soldiers made, they helped to keep this country free.

- Mark Henley, AeroShell Team

The AeroShell Aerobatic Team is always a show favorite, as the big AT-6 Texans scribe their paths with smoke.

PATTY WAGSTAFF

Anytime you get to fly a P-51 Mustang, it is a good day. Anytime you get to fly one in an airshow is an even better day.

I was one of the lucky individuals to fly *Princess Elizabeth*, a rare C model recently imported from England. During my first flight in her, I realized she was faster and cleaner than the P-51Ds I had flown. Not only was I flying a rare piece of history, but also I was in for a treat when it came to flying the show.

There were many World War II Veteran P-51 pilots and crewmembers at The Gathering, and I wanted to make sure to honor the WASPs and their contributions. My airshow performance was dedicated to them. I chose the Leonard Cohen song "Hallelujah" to fly to because while the song is about women, to me its lyrics also speak to the P-51. Normally I don't listen to music when performing, but at The Gathering I did and was able to fly to the rhythm of the song.

In addition to flying *Princess Elizabeth*, I started the day flying the airshow with my Cirrus-sponsored Extra 300S. As one Mustang pilot put it, vaudeville in the morning and the main event in the afternoon. I kind of liked that analogy!

- *Patty Wagstaff*

Patty Wagstaff's Extra 300S is a common sight at airshows around the country. Her long career as an aerobatic performer has given her a distinction as one of the world's top aviators.

MICHAEL GOULIAN

Quite simply, The Gathering of Mustangs and Legends defined the 2007 airshow season. If you were anyone in the North American airshow scene, you just had to be there.

The event paid tribute to an amazing machine. To see the spectacle of so many Mustangs in the air and to witness the emotion in the eyes of the warriors who made them famous was a feeling I will never forget. To fly in honor of and in front of the Legends themselves gave me a good case of stage fright. When I retire from flying airshows, The Gathering will be one of my fondest memories. The weather, the planes, and the people were all inspirational.

- Michael Goulian

T-6 TEXAN

It wasn't until I arrived that I realized just how special this event would be.

I was standing next to a veteran as a Mustang was starting and he said "only a Merlin has that characteristic smell." It was then that I knew just what this event meant to so many.

It was an honor and a pleasure flying the T-6 solo performance and being able to display the "Texan" in front of all of those who learned to fly in it.

- Eric Fazier, T-6 demo pilot

THE HORSEMEN

There are few events that stick in your memory, no matter how far time takes you from them. The 2007 Gathering is such an event. Fortunately, the show occurred in 2007, permitting me time to bring the P-51C *Princess Elizabeth*. Having it play such an integral part of the show, such as the opening ceremonies, formation aerobatics, the F-22 Heritage Flight, and the Final 51, was a highlight for me. Time has taken us from 2007, but the photos, videos, and memories will never fade.

- Jimmy Beasley, Horsemen lead

P-51 FLIGHT DEMONSTRATION

I was extremely proud to be part of The Gathering of Mustangs and Legends celebration, which pulled so much history together for four special days in Columbus, Ohio.

As a small boy in Central Florida, I first watched R. A. "Bob" Hoover fly the P-51 Mustang at a local airshow. I was in awe, not only with the power and performance of this incredible aircraft, but also with the ability of the pilot. Who could imagine almost 50 years later I would have the privilege to fly the Mustang as a tribute to Mr. Hoover and so many of the other Legends? I was truly humbled to have a chance to bring the Mustang to life once again for these Legends and the hundreds of thousands of people who attended the event.

I have been blessed to be able to fly the Mustang almost every day for well over 20 years, flights not in hostile skies but rather enjoyable flights in peaceful times. From my roll on take-off to the last maneuver, my Mustang flight demonstration was a tribute to these brave men and women who helped write a special chapter in history, a chapter written in blood defending our freedom.

- Lee Lauderback, P-51 demo pilot

RED BARON PIZZA SQUADRON

I remember clearly the first morning after our early briefing. We began pre-flighting the trainers at our station on the far northeast end of the field, surrounded by lush green countryside. You could smell the avgas and dew coming together on a beautiful fall morning. Then the stillness was broken by an unmistakable sound as a flight of two Mustangs appeared, raked overhead, and vanished as we strained to focus on their details, imagining we were amongst them. Most of us dreamed of flying Mustangs, and they always turned our heads. We were in awe as flights of two, three, and four growled overhead, returning from dawn patrols. For a moment, it was 1944 and we had that same look that I saw all week in the eyes of our Legends striding proudly and vigorously through this "Gathering" of so many of their old mounts and comrades. The scene had seemingly erased the 60 or so years of wear and tear from those well-traveled faces. They were once again strong with knowledge, wisdom, and elevated respect. Never had I participated in such an honorable event. It was unlike anything we had ever experienced, and we were all graciously inspired.

- Bryan Regan, Red Baron Pizza Squadron pilot

The Air National Guard is a formidable training ground for a variety of aircraft. This pilot is strutting the ANG's stuff.

AIR NATIONAL GUARD

To see the massive numbers of aviation enthusiasts of all ages show their gratitude to our veterans for service to their country left an impression in my heart that will last a lifetime. The event allowed each and every one of us in attendance to stop for a moment and reflect on those who could not be with us to celebrate this momentous occasion because they had made the ultimate sacrifice.

The sheer number of both airplanes and attendees was a testament to this great country's patriotism and pride. It was an honor and a privilege to be just a small part of that.

- Lt. Col. John Klatt, Air National Guard (ANG) Aerobatic Team

JOHN MOHR

I was honored to be invited to perform in The Gathering of Mustangs and Legends. The show exceeded my expectations by a long shot. Watching the WWII veterans who attended and interacted with the crowds, listening to them tell their stories or take a moment to explain a particular characteristic of their Mustangs…it touched my heart in a way that no other venue could. These men and women were bigger than life. As I watched the Mustangs being flown in solo and formation maneuvers, it instilled a sense of pride to be born and raised in the greatest country on earth. The Gathering of Mustangs and Legends was THE show of the decade and possibly the best in the last 25 years.

- John Mohr

AIR FORCE RESERVE

I was honored to be a part of such a historic event. I appreciate that honor now more than ever. However, I didn't fully realize how special it really was until several years later. Besides flying airshows, I still fly F-16s and got promoted to Lieutenant Colonel. Recently, I was studying in Air War College and the first course required me to study the air campaigns of both Europe and the Pacific during World War II. I always knew the P-51 was a great airplane, but after detailed study, I see that now more than ever. Since the GML, I realized it was one airplane that made the difference in WWII. I hope that I helped draw more attention to the heroes of the GML – the pilots, their patriotism, and their magnificent Mustangs.

- Ed Hamil, Air Force Reserve

The Air Force Reserve is as demanding as active duty. This pilot demonstrates that not all the Reserve's flying is tactical.

ALMOST REAL

If you're a newcomer to the warbird community, you might be surprised at the effort that is put into the detail. Aircraft are painstakingly researched to learn where a fuel line makes that now essential turn, exactly what letters and numbers were where, how the main gear tuck into their wells…for some, aircraft that are not original, or at least authentic, are just not quite right.

The lust for authenticity is pervasive, if not downright infectious. Pilots in vestigial battle uniforms and vintage jeeps speeding along the taxiways, everywhere there was evidence of the largest war effort ever conceived and executed. "Getting it right" is considered a rite of passage.

The Gathering of Mustangs and
Legends was enhanced by the
authenticity and abundance of
period clothing and accessories.

The purpose behind the massive effort to create the Gathering of Mustangs and Legends was simply to see, feel, smell, touch, and hear the magic of the P-51 and to pay homage to men and women whose lives were touched by that amazing airplane. Everyone seemed to understand that. Except maybe the Legends themselves.

"It was very satisfying and amazing to see the interest of so many young people," wrote World War II Mustang pilot James Herbert.

Robert "Punchy" Powell said, "Although we don't think of ourselves as heroes, The Gathering made us all feel like we were. It brought back memories of the days of our youth when we were blessed with the opportunity to fly and fight for our country in the best fighter of the time. What more could we ever ask for in our lifetime?"

The 51 Legends attending the event were honored by a special "51" formation flyover, which required a significant amount of planning and development by flight directors and pilots.

THE MUSTANGS

The North American P-51 Mustang was the most successful fighter in World War II and is the most recognized warbird in the world. Many say this was the airplane that turned the tide toward Allied air superiority. But that didn't come easy. The 8th, 9th, and 15th Air Forces' P-51 groups shot down 4,950 aircraft (almost 50 percent of all USAAF claims in the European Theater) and the most claimed by any Allied fighter in air-to-air combat.

YOU OUGHTA BE IN PICTURES

A huge hangar at Rickenbacker was also transformed into a large photo studio, big enough to capture a distinct image of every Mustang attending. It was hard to miss because of the Hollywood-style lighting blaring out of the open hangar door.

A young girl on her daddy's shoulder stood watching several men prepare the next aircraft for its portrait.

"Daddy, is this like the Super Bowl?" she asked.

Her father smiled and thought a moment. "Well, yes, it is," he answered her.

And in fact, the events are comparable with respect to the amount of effort that goes on long before game time.

A number of venues for The Gathering of Mustangs and Legends were selected across the United States. Each preliminary possibility had to be evaluated for a number of important factors and then thoroughly researched. Once the Air Force determined it wanted to conduct Heritage Flights in conjunction with the event, other requirements, including security concerns (America's most advanced fighter, the F-22, was coming) and acceptable runway lengths had to be considered.

It was determined that the owners of all airworthy North American P-51 Mustangs would be invited.

A list of Legends, from pilots to crews, needed to be created, then refined to the top 51 men and women who best represented

the Mustang and its accomplishments. Current locations for the Legends had to be investigated before the formal invitations could even be sent. Complete arrangements for transportation to the event and suitable accommodations would need to be made more than a year in advance.

There were civilian airshow performers who would need to align their schedules to attend.

The Air Force would need to shape their presence and requirements specific to the venue.

As word of this once in a lifetime event sped around the world-wide aviation community, the media became obsessed.

Hundreds of journalists, reporters, photographers, and videographers, including those from the BBC, PBS, and even major motion picture studios, began to apply for credentials to attend.

It all led to this moment – bright lights, a piece of American history, and more lives impacted by the P-51 Mustang.

"All these lights make the airplane so shiny," the little girl told her father.

"Yes, honey, isn't that cool?" her father asked.

Ain't Misbehavin'

N51KB • P-51D-25NA • Jim Thompson, Wes Stowers,
William Strickland, & Dr. Evan Zeiger

Ain't Misbehavin' served in the Royal Canadian Air Force from 1945 to 1957. After 1957, the plane passed through civilian hands. One owner, Bill McGrath, named the plane *Kat Bird* in 2001. In 2006, the aircraft was purchased by a group called the Mustang Pilots, LLC and they renamed her *Ain't Misbehavin'.* They operate her regularly out of Birmingham International Airport in Alabama.

The current *Ain't Misbehavin'* is tribute to the original P-51D given the name by pilot Jesse R. Frey of the 357th Fighter Group.

> "It was indeed a high honor to have been present to witness this magnificent occasion...one Legend of the 357th Group, with a tear in his eye and a heart filled with gratitude, told me it was a crowning moment in his life."
>
> **Jim Thompson**

American Beauty was reborn in 1968, a product of the Cavalier Aircraft Corp., a Florida-based company famous for refurbishing P-51D Mustangs.

American Beauty

N151MC • P-51D-Cavalier • John O'Connor

This Mustang was refurbished by Cavalier Aircraft Corporation in 1968. Later she was acquired by Ross Grady of Canada and renamed *What's Up Doc*. Max Chapman purchased the aircraft in 1998 and restored it as *American Beauty*. The plane was sold in 2007 to John O'Connor.

Barbara Jean   N10607 • P-51D-30NA • Harry Barr

Barbara Jean suffered an off-field landing in 2005 and sustained extensive wing and fuselage damage. The aircraft was then restored by Bob Odegaard and was returned to service.

Before she was *Barbara Jean*, she raced in Reno as *Georgia Mae*. Earlier Jack Slaker owned her and used the aircraft in a number of high performance, cross-country races. This Mustang was built near the end of World War II in 1945. Later she saw service in Canada. She fell back into civilian hands and was lovingly refurbished starting in 1993 by new owner Harry Barr.

Betty Jane

N251MX • TF-51C-10NT • Max C. Chapman Jr.

Betty Jane is the only full dual-cockpit TF-51C in existence today. Craig Charleston recovered the original components for this restoration from Southern England, and John Muszala of Pacific Fighters started the restoration in 2000. May 5, 2004, she made her first flight, and in this same year took home the trophy for Best P-51 Mustang at EAA AirVenture in Oshkosh, Wisconsin. In 2006, she was repainted in the paint scheme of the 31st Fighter Group, 307th Fighter Squadron and named *Betty Jane*.

Only a handful of the original B/C models of the P-51 still exist today. During World War II, several of these models were modified to have a rear seat. General Dwight Eisenhower sat in the back of a P-51C, while overseeing the battles on the beaches of Normandy during the D-Day invasion. This airplane's markings are a tribute to the 31st Fighter Group.

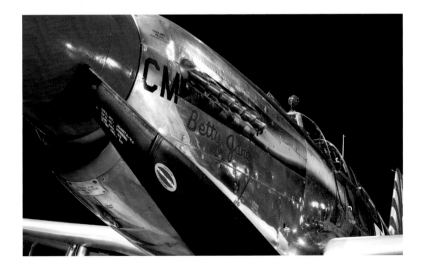

The original *Big Beautiful Doll* was flown by Col. John Landers, one of the most famous aces from World War II. Landers was an ace in both the Pacific and European Theaters. Restored in 1992, this P-51's cockpit is a combination of both new and original features.

Big Beautiful Doll

N351BD • P-51D-20NA • Mike Henningsen

Big Beautiful Doll was restored by Pacific Fighters and owned and flown by Ed Shipley for over nine years. Mr. Henningsen purchased the plane in 2003, and she wears the paint scheme of Colonel John Landers from when he commanded the 78th Fighter Group. Colonel Landers destroyed approximately 14 planes in the air and over 20 on the ground.

Boomer N94384 • P-51D-30NA • Tim McPherson

Boomer originally belonged to Tim McPherson's brother from 1975 to 1977 and was then sold to Max Hoffman of Ft. Collins, Colorado. The plane burned in a hangar fire in 1981, but Tim McPherson ended up with *Boomer's* original paperwork. *Boomer's* assembly began October 21, 1988 with a collection of parts, and 18 years later on July 17, 2006 *Boomer* flew after much collecting and rebuilding.

At one time, *Boomer* was flown by air racer Mickey Rupp, who's credited with saying, "Air racing may not be better than your wedding night, but it's better than the second night!"

Cavalier Aircraft Corp. restored a number of war surplus P-51 Mustangs for governments and private individuals worldwide. Some of the aircraft projects were purchased from scrap dealers who intended to melt the Mustangs down.

Cavalier   N51DL • P-51D-5NA • Edward & David B. Lindsay

This aircraft was modified in 1944 for high-speed research testing by NACA. Mustang 44-13257 made 87 flights. "Tests were conducted up to .82 mach, the highest speed ever attained by any F-51D," according to John F. Reeder of NACA. In 1957, it sold for $931.00. In 1967, Cavalier Aircraft Corp. remanufactured the plane using it as a demonstrator/test/chase aircraft as well as a weapons testing platform for the U.S. Army. Since 1972, it has been used as a personal aircraft of the Lindsay family.

Checkertail Clan

N1451D • P-51D-30NA • Nathan Davis

Starting in 1950, Mustang 44-74446 served in the Royal Canadian Air Force. From 1960 to 1970 the fighter had Canadian civil registration, and from 1970 to present has had registration with various U.S. owners. The plane was wrecked three times and had its last full ground-up restoration in 1995. The current owner purchased *Checkertail Clan* in 2001 and in 2003 it was painted as #11 as flown by Major H. H. "Herky" Green, the highest scoring 325th ace with 18 total kills, five in the Mustang.

As *Unruly Julie* this P-51D crashed in Arizona in 1987, then again at the Reno Air Races in 1994. After an immaculate restoration, she's now flying as *Checkertail Clan.*

The big four-bladed propeller is a component of the magical sound of *Cincinnati Miss'* 1180 HP V-1650-7 Rolls-Royce engine.

Cincinnati Miss

N83KD • P-51D-25NT • David O'Maley

Manufactured in 1944 as P-51D-25-NT, this plane was designated a Mustang IV and exported to the Royal Australian Air Force in 1945. Stephen Wilmans acquired the plane in the 1990s and started a complete restoration led by Aero Trader of Chino, California. After Mr. Wilmans' death in 2002, Stars & Bars completed the project in 2005. *Cincinnati Miss* is painted to represent the 353rd Fighter Group, 350th Fighter Squadron based in Raydon, England in 1944-45. Currently she is operated by the Tri-State Warbird Museum based at the Clermont County Airport in Batavia, Ohio.

This aircraft was born in 1944, then remanufactured by the Cavalier Aircraft Corp. in the 1960s. Since then she has gone through a series of major restorations and now flies as *Cincinnati Miss*. She sports the paint scheme of the 353rd Fighter Group based in Raydon, England where she served with the RCAF.

City of Winnipeg Sqdn.

N63476 • P-51D-20NA • Bob May

Delivered to the Army Air Force in 1944, the *City of Winnipeg Sqdn.* was shipped to the Mediterranean Theater but eventually returned to the United States. It was sold to the Uruguay Air Force in 1949. Lost in a training accident in 1952 and salvaged from the lake it rested in for 50 years in 1995, it was sent for reconstruction in North Dakota and saw completion in 2004. The post-war Royal Canadian Air Force paint scheme is from an actual City of Winnipeg Squadron Aircraft.

Cloud Dancer has gone through a number of loving hands since her manufacture in 1944. After many years as an air racer, she now lives at the Leeward Air Ranch in Florida, a 500-acre private mecca for warbird lovers the world over.

Cloud Dancer

N55JL • P-51D-25NT • Jimmy Leeward

Mustang 44-84615 served in the Swiss and Israeli Air Forces until 1966. In 1974, Jimmy Leeward purchased and restored the plane. It flew in the movies *Cloud Dancer, Smokey and The Bandit Part 3, Tuskegee Airmen*, and *Thunder Over Reno*. At 16 in 1979, Dirk Leeward made his first solo flight in *Cloud Dancer* and raced it in Reno in 1986, participating in the first father-son Unlimited racing team with his father flying the *Galloping Ghost. Cloud Dancer* currently serves as the goodwill ambassador for Leeward Air Ranch.

Crazy Horse

N851D • TF-51D-25NT • Lee Lauderback

Crazy Horse was sold surplus in 1957 as a P-51D. David Lindsay of Cavalier Aircraft Corp. took the stock single seat airframe and modified her to dual cockpit/dual control TF-51 standards. This was the last TF-51 off the Cavalier production line. In 1984, Bob Byrnes purchased her from Bob Amyx and named the plane *Rascal III*. Doug Schultz and Lee Lauderback purchased the plane in 1987 and once again changed her name to *Crazy Horse*. The aircraft was painted in the colors of the 352nd Fighter Group, 487th Fighter Squadron, 8th Air Force based at Asch, Belgium. Today, *Crazy Horse* is one of the most recognizable Mustangs in existence, having trained hundreds of Mustang pilots, provided orientation flights to thousands, and thrilled millions at airshows around the country.

Crazy Horse is the flagship aircraft for Stallion 51, the world's foremost Mustang facility located in Kissimmee, Florida. With her dual controls, this plane has trained many a pilot and introduced thousands to the unique experience of flying the P-51.

Crazy Horse² levels off in preparation for a roll on takeoff as a salute to R. A. "Bob" Hoover.

Crazy Horse²

N351DT • TF-51D-30NA • Lee Lauderback

Crazy Horse² served in the Royal Canadian Air Force from 1950 to 1960 and was then released into civilian hands. The aircraft was highly modified in the early 1970s and raced by Ken Burnstine as #34 Miss Foxy Lady. John Crocker acquired the aircraft in 1978, racing it as Sumthin' Else until its 1990 crash landing. In 1997, Dick Thurman purchased and rebuilt the aircraft as a dual-controlled TF-51, naming it Kentucky Babe. It won Best P-51 at Oshkosh 2000. In 2005, Stallion 51 purchased the aircraft and repainted it like the original Crazy Horse.

This blue nose design was originally made famous by Major George E. Preddy, Jr. of the 328th Fighter Squadron, 352nd Fighter Group. Preddy is credited 26.83 air-to-air victories. He was killed flying the original Cripes A' Mighty (above, right) on Christmas Day 1944.

Cripes A' Mighty 3rd

N921 • P-51D-30NT • Kermit Weeks

Kermit Weeks observes "We all fly in our dreams and soar in our imaginations," which prompted him to open Fantasy of Flight in Central Florida, home to this unprecedented two-time Grand Champion Warbird at Oshkosh (1987 and 1999). Painted in tribute to Mustang top ace Major George E. Preddy's legendary *Cripes A' Mighty 3rd*, this D model has undergone two total restorations, the first taking authenticity of a warbird to a new level, and the second to an even higher level following Hurricane Andrew's 1992 devastation of the Weeks Air Museum in Miami. Originally built in 1945, but too late to enter the war, it resided with the New Zealand Royal Air Force until 1958, when it passed into civilian hands and flew in the New Zealand airshow circuit as the *Mobil Mustang*. It returned to the States in 1974, and Kermit Weeks acquired it in 1978.

Cripes A' Mighty

N151BW • P-51D-30NA • Bill Wiemann

Cripes A' Mighty USAAF Serial #44-74813 is a tribute to Major G. E. Preddy of the 352nd Fighter Group, "The Blue-Nosed Bastards of Bodney." Major Preddy is ranked as the third highest scoring ace in the European Theater of Operations, the seventh highest scoring American ace, and the top P-51 Mustang ace with 26.83 aerial victories. Midwest Aero Restorations completed a no-expense-spared restoration in 2002, including gun sites, guns, and ammunition and won the Grand Champion Warbird World War II Award at FAA AirVenture.

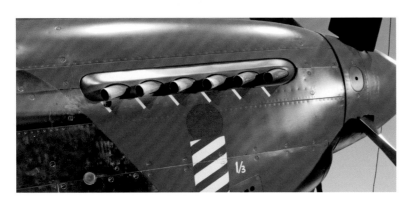

Dakota Kid II

N151HR • P-51D-30NA • Hank Reichert

Dakota Kid II is an actual 8th Air Corps plane that went to Sweden after the war, and later to the Dominican Republic, before it was brought to the States and restored. The aircraft is finished in the markings of a plane flown by a North Dakota veteran, Noble Peterson, who flew two tours of duty with the 355th Fighter Group, 358th Fighter Squadron. The plane also carries the mark of the crew chief, Robert Coleman, of Long Island, New York.

The original *Dakota Kid* was a C model, named such because the pilot was the only flyer in the 355th Fighter Group from North Dakota. The yellow nose and tail feathers marked the 358th Fighter Squadron. Its primary mission was bomber escort and low level strafing.

DF-X   N20TF • TF-51D Cavalier MKII • Dan Friedkin

In 1967, Mustang 67-14866 was acquired by Cavalier Aircraft Corporation and served as a part of Operation Peace Condor. The Bolivian Air Force obtained the plane in 1968, and it then went to Canada in 1977 under civilian ownership. The plane passed through several different owners, one of whom crashed in Texas. It was restored in 2001 in Chino and in 2004 was painted in the 78th Fighter Group colors. Later, it was shipped to the UK for the Duxford show, but has since returned to the U.S.

The checkerboard nose belongs to the 78th Fighter Group assigned during World War II to RAF Duxford. Originally part of the 8th Air Force, the fighter group was deactivated in 1945, but not before claiming 338 kills in the air and 358 ground aircraft destroyed.

DiamondBack

N51ZM • TF-5ID-30NT • Mark Peterson

DiamondBack is a dual cockpit TF-51 Mustang built in 1945 that served in the U.S. military. Private owners flew the aircraft from 1958 until 1979. In 1984, a team rebuilt her into the racer *Stiletto*. Skip Holm flew her to first place in the Unlimited Gold race in 1984 at 437.6 mph. In 1993, Pete Regina restored her to a "stock" TF-51 Mustang. Stallion 51 Maintenance put the finishing touches on the aircraft in 1998 and painted her in a 356th Fighter Group, 360th Fighter Squadron scheme.

"It's impossible to describe my feelings about The Gathering with words. The finest aviation event ever produced. I was honored just to be there."

Mark Peterson

DiamondBack has been restored to full dual cockpit/dual control TF-51 standards. The cockpit has been modernized with a state of the art avionics package, which reduces pilot workload in today's complex airspace system.

Double Trouble Two N7TF • P-51D-20NA • Tom Friedkin

Double Trouble Two was owned by Jim Jeffers in 1963 and was race #83. That same year Contractor Equipment Sales acquired the aircraft. In 1966, the aircraft was sold to Fowler Aeronautical Services who owned it until purchased by Air Carriers, Inc. in 1969. That same year it changed hands again to Gale Aero Corp. and was registered as N711UP. In 1976, Tom Friedkin of Cinema Air, Inc. purchased the aircraft and changed the registration to N7TF. A restoration was started in 2005 and completed in 2007 when she was painted in the marking of the 353rd Fighter Group and named *Double Trouble Two*.

Double Trouble Two has flown with the three-airplane Horsemen Aerobatic Team, the world's only P-51 Mustang aerobatic team. Their airshow routine has the aircraft performing to a musical score.

Double Trouble Two N51EA • P-51D-20NA • Jerry Yagen

After its completion in 1945, this aircraft was shipped to England. Sold to Sweden in 1947, and later to Nicaragua, it returned to the U.S. in 1963. It changed ownership from there, possibly flying for El Salvador in the July 1969 Soccer War. In 1982, it was painted in its *Double Trouble Two* markings; black and yellow checkers on the nose, representing "Wild Bill Bailey's" aircraft of the 353rd Fighter Group. It flew in Reno from 1983 to 1985 and won the Grand Champion award at the 1986 Sun n' Fun airshow.

Dusty's Dolly   N201F • P-51D-25NT • Doug Matthews

Dusty's Dolly sold as surplus in 1957 and was bought by Earl Dakin. She transferred through several civilian owners between the years of 1958 and 1969. In 1969, Suffolk Flight Association acquired the plane and flew it for almost a decade. In 1978, the fighter was purchased by John Mark who flew the airplane for almost 20 years until he sold it to Harry Barr in 2005. Doug Matthews purchased *Dusty's Dolly* in 2007.

With her D-Day stripes and polished aluminum, *Dusty Dolly* is a good example of what the P-51 looked like during World War II.

Excalibur

N151W • P-51D-30NT • Jim Read

Built in 1945, this P-51 served in the North Dakota, Alabama, and Kentucky Air National Guards. The aircraft was then sold to Dr. Jim Michaels, who named it *Queen B* and raced it in the Reno Air Races. Jim Read bought the plane in 1998 and it is kept in the Indiana Aviation Museum in Valparaiso, Indiana. *Excalibur* performs aerobatic routines, Heritage Flights, and static displays in numerous airshows around the country.

Though this cockpit is original in many ways, like so many Mustangs, it has been modernized. Unlike the original warbirds, this P-51 can fly an ILS.

Lt. James Brooks flew a P-51B named *January*, the month of his birth. He transitioned into the P-51D and named this aircraft *February*. Brooks was credited with 13 kills, the third highest in the 31st Fighter Group. He was awarded the Silver Star in August 1944.

"Those of us fortunate enough to own and fly one of these revered airplanes are the keepers of the flame."

Chris Woods

February

N351MX • P-51D-30NA • Chris Woods

North American manufactured 44-74391 in 1945 and it was delivered to 4003rd USAAF Base Unit Technical Service Command, New Jersey. From 1947 to 1955, it served as a National Air Guard airplane. In 1958, it was sold to the Guatemalan Air Force, returning to the U.S. in 1972 and owned by Don Hull. After passing through several owners, it was restored to flying condition in 2000 when Woods Aviation, LLC bought the plane and painted it in the wartime markings of Ace Lieutenant Jim Brooks of the 31st Fighter Group, 307th Fighter Squadron.

FF-704 N6168C • P-51D-25NA • Lewis Shaw

Produced in 1944 in California by North American, 44-73704 sold at surplus to Mather Air Force Base in 1957 for $1,000. In 1969, M. L. "Lefty" Gardener began a 24-year history performing in airshows and air races. Named *Thunderbird*, this plane and pilot won at the 1976 Reno Air Races taking the Gold Cup in the Unlimited class. In 1993 Ezell Aircraft Aviation bought and completely rebuilt the plane to the highest level of restoration, recreating the spirit of the last Mustang serving in the U.S. Air Force in 1958.

In 2001, this aircraft won the Preservation Award at AirVenture in Oshkosh, Wisconsin. She's seen here with her long range drop tanks and complete 1950s-vintage armament.

"These Legends and their victories are dimming; however they will remain part of our lives, as bright as our nation's history and heritage. With now so few, we are just beginning to understand how missed they will be when they are gone. That is why I was at The Gathering."

Lewis Shaw

Flying Dutchman

N51AB • P-51D/CA-18 MK • Stephen Craig

Mustang A68-100 was the 100th Commonwealth Mustang built in Australia under license from North American Aviation. She was imported to the U.S. in 1967, adopting the registration N51AB and serial number 44-14777 in 1971. In 1990 the craft was sold to Norman Lewis and re-painted in the markings of Bob Goebel's *Flying Dutchman* of the 31st Fighter Group. In 1944, Goebel made his last Mustang flight having accumulated 303 hours of combat flying in 61 missions. Most recently the plane was purchased by Stephen Craig of Kansas in 2006.

Gentleman Jim

N551J • P-51D-30NA • Jack Roush

Up until 1963, when this Mustang was acquired by Bob Bixler, little is known of its past. From 1966 to 1972 it passed through various owners, but in 1973 its owner, David Norland, named the plane *No Name Dame* racer #76. In 2000, Jack Roush acquired the plane, and restoration began. It was completed in 2003 and the restored plane saw its first flight that August. In 2005, the name changed to *Gentleman Jim* to honor Captain Jim Browning.

Captain Jim Browning flew the original. He failed to return from an escort mission and was listed as missing in action in 1945, two missions short of completing his second tour of duty. Captain Browning's decorations include three Distinguished Flying Crosses, the Purple Heart, eight Air Medals, and the French Croix de guerre.

The red rudder illustrates the markings of the 357th Fighter Group based in England. Post-war, the 357th was one of the units chosen to form part of the occupation forces, moving to Neubiberg, Germany on July 21, 1945 where they remained until August 20, 1946.

Geraldine is a replica of Lieutenant Colonel Charles Roscoe "Chuck" Cummins' Mustang, named *Geraldine* after his wife.

Geraldine   N5500S • P-51D-30NA • Chuck & Bev Greenhill

In 1950 this Mustang was delivered to the RCAF, and in 1957 it fell into U.S. civilian hands. In 1961, it was sold as scrap and used as an outside display at a car dealership in New York. From 1965 to 1978 it passed through different owners, but was eventually restored to a World War II configuration. In 2001, she saw her first flight since restoration, piloted by Tim McCarter, and in 2002, she rolled out of the paint shop as *Geraldine*.

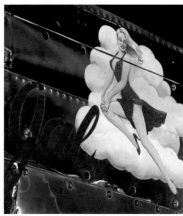

Glamorous Gal wears the markings of the 4th Fighter Group. When war broke out, American pilots volunteered to fly for the RAF, and because of their origins, were referred to as the Eagle Squadrons. When the United States entered the war, the Eagle Squadrons were consolidated into the 4th Fighter Group.

Glamorous Gal   N751RB • P-51D-30NA • Bob & Chris Baranaskas

Glamorous Gal has been flying with Warbirds Over Long Island of Brookhaven, New York since 2002. *Glamorous Gal* wears the colors of the 4th Fighter Group, formed from the famed Eagle Squadrons, and was the first fighter group of the 8th Air Force to penetrate German airspace on July 28, 1943. Bob and Chris Baranaskas of Warbirds Over Long Island proudly attended The Gathering of Mustangs and Legends to honor the integrity and bravery of the men and women of the Armed Forces who fought for the greater good and flew these incredible machines.

"Attendance for me was not optional —
I would be there with *Glamorous Glen III*
come proverbial hell or high water...
It was an honor I'll never forget."

Mark Huffstutler

Glamorous Glen III   N3333E • P-51D-20NA • Mark Huffstutler

Built originally as P-51D-20NA, it was delivered to the RCAF in June of 1947. She served with the RCAF until September 1960. She served as a gate guard to the RCAF Lincoln Park, Alberta from 1960 until 1962. Sold into civilian hands and rebuilt in the early 1960s, David Tallichet acquired her in 1969. In 2001, she was sold to Wayne Rudd who operated her under the same name. Mark became her custodian in 2004.

GunFighter is painted as an aircraft from the 343rd Fighter Squadron, which actively flew combat sorties in the European Theater during the last year and a half of the war. The 343rd has morphed into a reconnaissance unit and is still active today.

GunFighter

N5428V • P-51D-25NA • Commemorative Air Force

P-51D, 44-73264 was built in March 1945 in North American's Inglewood, California plant and shipped to Europe. In July 1945, she returned to the United States and was assigned to Olmstead Army Airfield in Harrisburg, Pennsylvania until 1947. She flew in Air National Guard units until she was declared surplus and sold on the civilian market in 1957. GunFighter is restored in the colors of the 343rd Fighter Squadron, 55th Fighter Group, 66th Fighter Wing, Wormingford, England, 1944-45.

This Mustang was proudly flown for 30 years by Brigadier General Reg Urschler (Ret.) and could be seen proudly presenting the American Flag while on display and taxiing.

Hell-er Bust is painted to depict 1st Lieutenant Edwin Heller's P-51 from the 486th Fighter Squadron, 352nd Fighter Group. Lieutenant Heller shot down 19 enemy aircraft in World War II. In the Korean War he was credited with 3.5 victories before being shot down and taken prisoner by the Chinese Communists.

Hell-er Bust   N7551T • P-51D-20NA • John Sessions

Delivered to the 8th Air Force in 1945, 44-72438 also served with the Swedish and Dominican Republic Air Forces. Brian O'Farrell of Johnson Aviation in Hialeah, Florida returned the plane to the United States and Mr. Selby R. Burch of Kissimmee, Florida acquired it. Once it was restored to flying condition, it claimed Grand Champion World War II Warbird at the 1997 Sun 'n Fun. Bob Jepson purchased the Mustang, flying it as *Lady Alice*, until 2000 when it was renamed *Hell-er Bust*. In 2006, John Sessions of the Historic Aircraft Foundation, Seattle, Washington acquired it.

Hi-G   N6306T • P-51D-30NA • Tom Wood

North American P51D-30NA, S/N 44-74878 was built in late 1944 and delivered to the Royal Canadian Air Force in January, 1951 as 9259. This Mustang entered civilian service in the United States as 44-74787 in February 1957. During the next 50 years, *Hi-G* was bought and sold six times until she landed in the hands of her current owner, Mr. Tom Wood, who purchased her in March 1969. In the early 1970s, Mr. Wood choose the 55th Fighter Group's paint scheme and dubbed her *Hi-G*.

Hi-G shows off the colors of the 55th Pursuit Group, renamed the 55th Fighter Group in 1942. The group flew long range escort missions during the "Big Week," a six-day period in which 8th Air Force Bombers flew more than 3,000 sorties against German aviation targets. The 15th Air Force, based in Italy, flew another 500+. Together they dropped more than 10,000 tons of bombs.

In 1944, Dr. Kent Mosley was alone and injured over Germany until Major Pete Peterson and his Mustang arrived, taking down two of three attacking ME-109s. Captain Mosley's only clue to identify his savior was *Hurry Home Honey* on the aircraft's nose. 60 years later Mosley and Peterson officially met for the first time at a Lexington airshow.

Hurry Home Honey

N3751D • P-51D-25NA • Dr. Joe Richardson

In the late 1960s Cavalier Aircraft Corp. in Sarasota, Florida rebuilt *Hurry Home Honey* as a Cavalier 2000 "High Speed Executive Transport." She wore a yellow and black civilian scheme. In 1975, she was shipped to Tahiti and flown sporadically until 1984. The aircraft was shipped to Chino, California where extensive maintenance was undertaken and the 357th Fighter Group paint scheme was applied. In 1985, Charles Osborne purchased N3751D. Osborne stored the plane until 1989, when Lee Lauderback ferried *Hurry Home Honey* to Florida to undertake another extensive IRAN by Peter and Richard Lauderback. In the early 1990s, *Hurry Home Honey* was reunited with Pete Peterson, the original pilot of the wartime aircraft. Over the subsequent years, *Hurry Home Honey* has attended many airshows across the country and flown in the USAF Heritage Flight program by Brad Hood. 2006 saw her sold to Dr. Joe Richardson, who continues to operate her as a tribute to the 357th and Pete Peterson.

Ina the Macon Belle   N1204 • P-51C-10NT • Kermit Weeks

This aircraft is one of two P-51Cs Paul Mantz purchased and modified to win the Bendix Transcontinental Race in 1948. Modifying the wings to hold 406 gallons of fuel allowed the aircraft to make the trip without using external tanks. Kermit Weeks acquired this aircraft in 1985 and is one of only four original P-51B/Cs remaining in the world. Mr. Weeks restored the plane to a military configuration, painting it in the red tail colors of the highest-scoring Tuskegee Airman Lee Archer, a friend of Mr. Weeks and a Fantasy of Flight enthusiast. Meticulously restored, it received the prestigious Grand Champion Warbird Award at the 2000 AirVenture in Oshkosh.

The red tail of this rare P-51C is tribute to the Tuskegee Airmen, formally the 332nd Fighter Group in the U.S. Army Air Corps. This racially segregated group of fighter pilots flew 15,533 combat sorties and 1,578 missions. The Tuskegee Airmen are credited with shooting down 112 German aircraft and destroying another 150 on the ground.

> "In the words of Mr. World War II USO himself, Bob Hope, 'Thanks for the memories!'"
>
> **Kermit Weeks**

During her first restoration, *La Pistolera* became a P-51 Mustang with a turboprop jet engine. The Rolls-Royce Dart made its debut right after World War II and ultimately became the chosen powerplant for a number of smaller airliners. The British continued producing the engine until the late 1980s.

La Pistolera N50FS • TF-51/CA MK.22 • Rod Lewis

This Mustang was delivered to the Royal Australian Air Force in 1950 and from there passed through numerous owners beginning in 1958. From 1961 to 1967, it was kept in open storage, and it wasn't until 1976 that restoration was attempted – a restoration with a Rolls-Royce Dart turboprop. In 1995, it returned to the U.S. to World Jet, Inc. In 2006, Rod Lewis named the plane *La Pistolera*.

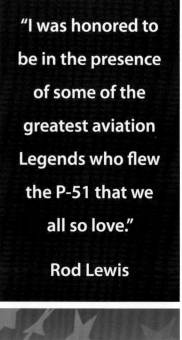

"I was honored to be in the presence of some of the greatest aviation Legends who flew the P-51 that we all so love."

Rod Lewis

La Pistolera, Spanish for "the holster," now flies with a standard Merlin engine.

Lady B   N151FT • P-51D-30NA • Fred Telling

Since her 1958 military retirement, Ed Weiner raced *Lady B* and in 1966 won first place at Los Angeles in the Unlimited Championship as race #49 with 375.81 mph. With further successful races, Ed secured the Bardahl sponsorship in 1968, returning to Reno as *Bardahl Miss*, with a yellow and black checkerboard paint scheme. Ed died in 1969, and in 1979 Max Hoffman bought and renamed the plane *Boomer II* and also raced successfully at Reno. In 2005, Fred Telling bought her from a French owner, reassembled her, rebuilt the engine, and renamed her *Lady B*.

La Pistolera Cockpit

Lady Jo N327DB • TF-51D-25NT • Daryl Bond

Lady Jo saw service with the Indonesian Air Force until sometime in the late 1970s. Eventually she made her way back to the United States, where John MacGuire owned her from 1984 until 1988. She was completely rebuilt into a TF-51D using a fuselage from the Enforcer Program and other spares. She has raced at Reno as Race #81 and is operated on a regular basis by her owner.

Lady Jo was cobbled together with fuselage components left over from the Enforcer Program, a short-lived attempt by the Cavalier Aircraft Company and ultimately the Piper Aircraft Company to develop the P-51 into the ultimate fighter. Despite ongoing efforts to sell the idea to the U.S. military as well as foreign governments, the Enforcer Program was a failure.

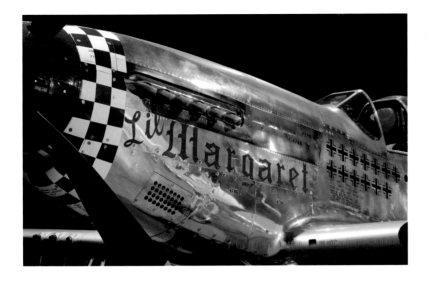

Lil' Margaret

N51BS • F-6D-25NT • Butch Schroeder

Lil' Margaret, a North American F-6D Mustang was accepted by the USAAF in 1945 and served with the 363rd TRS at Brooks Field, Texas in 1946. Michael Coutches stored 44-84756 from 1952 until 1961 when Bill Myers bought her and stored her for a further twenty years until Henry "Butch" Schroeder of Danville, Illinois acquired her in 1981. The aircraft was restored in the markings of Clyde East's *Lil' Margaret* and she made her first flight in 1993. Taken to Oshkosh in 1993, *Lil' Margaret* was awarded Grand Champion.

Lil' Margaret is a recreation of Capt. Clyde B. East's P-51 Mustang. He notched 13 air-to-air victories including one kill on D-Day, shooting down one of only four German aircraft destroyed that day.

As the war wound down in late 1944, North American Aviation, producer of the Mustang, found itself with extra airplanes. *Little Horse* was one such aircraft. Shortly after this aircraft was made, NAA sold the rights to the P-51 to Cavalier Aircraft Company.

> "It was also remarkable to hear the stories from the veterans, told not only with words but by the expressions on their faces and the reflection in their eyes."
>
> **Paul Ehlen**

Little Horse   N51PE • P-51D-30NT • Paul Ehlen

Little Horse came from the last group of 200 Mustangs produced by the NAA Texas plant in 1944. It was sold to the government as surplus in 1957, and its location until Walter Oakes bought it in 1963 is unknown. After Oakes, it went through several owners, and in 1983, Lynn Florey repainted it as *Death Rattler*. Harry Tope fatally crashed the plane in an Ottawa airshow. Gerry Beck obtained the wreckage and created a new P-51D in 1996. This plane was sold to Paul Ehlen, named *Little Horse*, and made its first flight in 2005.

Little Witch

N6320T • TF-51D-30NA • Bob Jepson

> "Memorable events, such as The Gathering of Mustangs and Legends, are the result of someone's vision, hard work, and dedication. We are all grateful to Lee Lauderback and his team for making this "once in a lifetime" Gathering a reality. This amazing event brought young and old together, the young to learn and the older to relive the majesty of the Mustang and its heroic pilots. Lee, from this grateful participant, heartfelt thanks."
>
> Bob Jepson

Mustang 44-74497 was delivered to the RCAF in 1950, then moved into civilian hands in 1958. It passed through several owners until it was acquired by Hess Bomberger in 1980 and operated as *Vergeltungswaffe*. In 1998, The Lady Alice Corporation purchased the plane and complete restoration ensued. This included restoring the wing panels and fuselage and assembling the aircraft using standards set forth by North American Aviation and Stallion 51 Maintenance. Repainted in the 353rd Fighter Group, 352nd Fighter Squadron scheme, she was named *Little Witch*, and awarded the Post World War II Grand Champion at Oshkosh 2003.

P-51D serial number 45-11391 was manufactured in 1945 and never saw action. She has, however, seen lots of action in private hands with registrations N6170C, N5151N, N51WT, N51MV, and names like *Nervous Energy* and now *Luscious Lisa*.

Luscious Lisa
N51MV • P-51D-30NT • Todd Stuart

Luscious Lisa has passed through a variety of owners. The first in 1963 was Thomas Drummond of California and from there she had several different owners and registrations. Her current owner is Todd Stuart who acquired the plane in 2006.

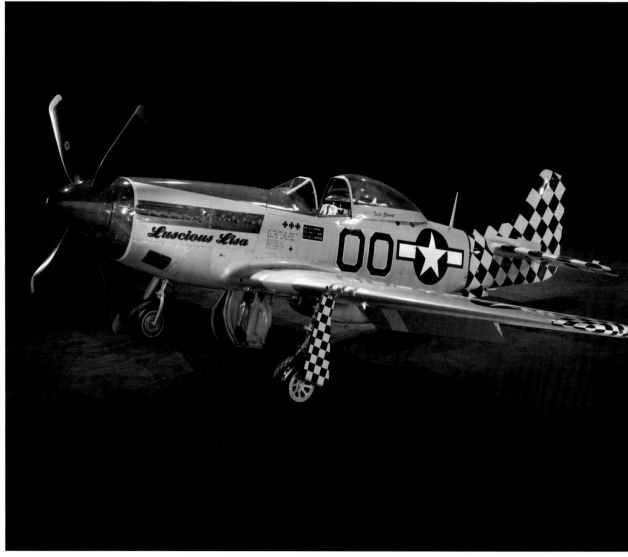

This aircraft sports the markings of the 55th Fighter Squadron which originally flew the P-38 Lightning over Europe. In 1944 the group switched to flying the P-51 Mustang.

Mad Max

N51MX • TF-51D-30NT • Max C. Chapman Jr.

The 55th Fighter Squadron flew their last mission in April 1945, and the squadron was demobilized after the war. It was reactivated a year later, however, and now flies the F-16 Fighting Falcon.

Mad Max is a dual cockpit/dual control Mustang built in 1945 as a P-51D-30NT. Converted to a Cavalier Mustang II in 1968 and delivered to the Salvadorian Air Force in 1969, it was returned to the U.S. in 1974 by Jack Flaherty. *Mad Max* wears the colors of Major Sam Brown of the 307th Fighter Squadron, 31st Fighter Group, 15th Air Force at Pomigliano, Italy. It is one of the sixteen operational dual-controlled Mustangs existing today.

"For me, The Gathering was the culmination of a lifetime interest and fascination with the P-51 Mustang and the generation of pilots who made it great."

Max Chapman

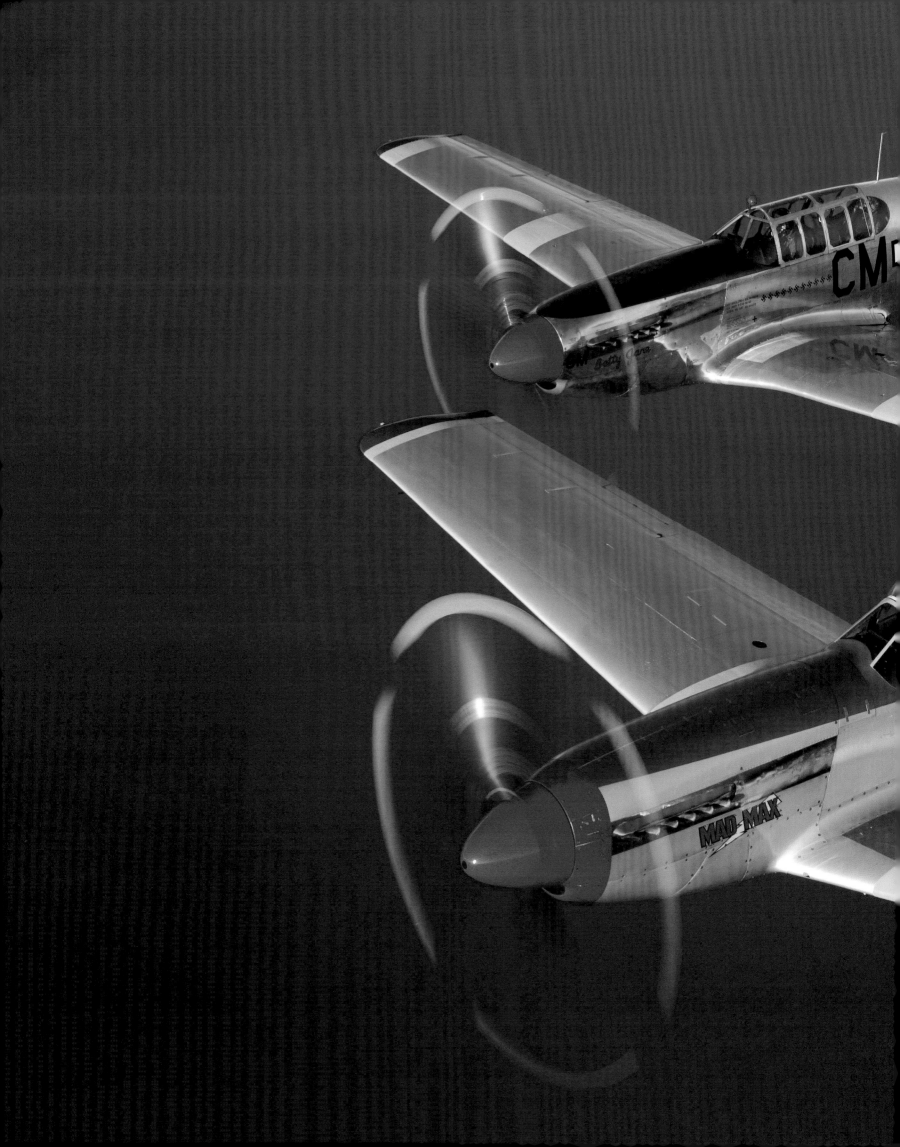

The Millie G

N551W • P-51D-10NA • Trent Latshaw

The Millie G was assigned to the 343rd Fighter Squadron, 55th Fighter Group, 8th Air Force. She was flown by Major Edward B. Giller, Commanding Officer. The airplane was named after his wife, Mildred.

The red nose of the 335th Fighter Group was originally an Eagle Squadron of the RAF and composed of American volunteer pilots. They were actively recruited by the English after heavy losses during the Battle of Britain in 1940.

The Miracle Maker   CF-IKE • P-51D-25NA • Ike Enns

Originally *The Widow Maker*, *The Miracle Maker* flew from Debden, England with the 335th 4th Fighter Group. After the war, it stayed in a U.S. compound in Sweden until it was acquired by Israel to help start their air force. Later, it rested in a school playground where kids played with it, and in the late 1970s Peter and Angelo Regina bought it. The P-51 belonged to Joe Kasperoff of California in 1983 until bought by Ike Enns, a Canadian citizen who flew it to Tulsa. It also races at Reno.

The white rudders outlined in red were markings of the 335th Fighter Group.

When German pilots got to examine the bubble canopy on the P-51D after the war, the revelation caused one pilot to say that the Luftwaffe would have done much better if they could have had that kind of visibility.

Miss Marilyn II

N41749 • P-51D-20NA • Christopher & Kit Goldsbury

Miss Marilyn II served in the Minnesota and Montana Air National Guard. In the late 1950s it was exported to Guatemala as FAG 354, and it returned to the U.S. in a group of seven planes purchased by partnership. Dick Hansen and Jeff Williams owned it in 1966 when she became *Miss Marilyn II*, an award-winning back to "stock" World War II configuration. With a desire to preserve the aircraft for history and honor the veterans who served our country, especially his friend "Tex" Hill, Christopher and Kit Goldsbury purchased *Miss Marilyn II* in 2004.

Though this airplane never saw combat duty during World War II, she has been restored to a perfect representation of the era.

> "Our decision to attend The Gathering in September 2007 was based upon our love for Mustangs, owning one, *Miss Marilyn II*, and thinking that it would be the last time to see P-51s in such a great number."
>
> **Kit Goldsbury**

Moonbeam McSwine

N2151D • P-51D-25NA • Vlado Lenoch

Moonbeam McSwine is the name given to the Mustang flown by World War II ace Captain William T. Whisner. The paint scheme depicts his war record of 18.5 victories over European skies. It served from 1968 to 1974 in the El Salvador Air Force. Upon its return, it was repainted as *Moonbeam McSwine* and won many awards as an early warbird recreation amongst the then usual white-civilian painted ex-military aircraft. *Moonbeam McSwine* continues flying around the Midwest at airshows and, most prominently, as a part of the USAF Heritage Flight.

Moonbeam McSwine is an example of "The Blue Nosed Bastards of Bodney," a paint scheme representing the 352nd Fighter Group.

Obsession   N651JM • P-51D-30NA • Jeffrey Michael

Delivered to the USAAF in 1945, she served with the 188th Fighter Squadron and was later flown by the 354th Fighter Squadron in Canada. She was then transferred to the 108th Fighter Squadron, O'Hare International Airport and later flown by the 169th Fighter Squadron, Illinois. In 1953, she was sold to the Indonesian Air Force, and in 1982, Ralph Johnson bought her and brought her back to the U.S. She was restored in Chino by Steve Hinton and Jim Maloney and sold in 1986 to Jeffrey Michael who named her *Obsession*.

This Mustang first flew with the 188th Fighter Squadron, now the 188th Fighter Wing flying F-16s based in New Mexico.

Old Crow

N6341T • P-51D-30NA • Jim Hagedorn

Old Crow was delivered to the RCAF in 1951 and found its way back stateside in 1962 when Margaret Kahlow acquired her. The plane passed through several owners until Jack Roush in1994, who gave her her current name, *Old Crow*. The plane's paint scheme is a tribute to the retired Colonel "Bud" Anderson. Jim Hagedorn acquired the plane in 2006.

"The Gathering of Mustangs and Legends was more than an airshow. It was a tribute to a generation of heroes and aircraft that changed the world – in fact saved it from evil. Throughout the planning process, all of us knew The Gathering was an event that would never be replicated. Given the rich history of military and civil aviation in Ohio, I'm proud to have played a role in bringing the event to Columbus and its deserving citizens. I am humbled to have been given the honor of flying my P-51 Mustang, Old Crow, above the tens of thousands of people who witnessed this epic event at Rickenbacker Air Force Base. While The Gathering is behind us, I hope we never forget why we gathered in the first place."

Jim Hagedorn

Ole Yeller, flown by R. A. "Bob" Hoover, may be the most recognizable of all Mustangs, having appeared in airshows across the United States and flown in Safety at Reno for 20 years. Hoover modified the aircraft's wing to hold an additional 320 gallons of fuel, allowing him to set a transcontinental speed record, coast to coast nonstop in five hours and 20 minutes. Hoover sold the airplane to friend John Bagley of Rexburg, Idaho in 1997.

Ole Yeller   N51RH • P-51D-30NA • John Bagley

This plane was bought in 1972 by Rockwell for Bob Hoover as a replacement for his aircraft that was damaged after an oxygen tank explosion. Bob flew the plane from 1972 to 1997 in airshow performances all over the U.S., Canada, and Mexico. Hoover also flew her at the Reno Air races until 1997 as the Safety Chase Plane, until it became evident this stock Mustang couldn't keep up with the racers. Its current owner, who flies the plane, houses *Ole Yeller* in the Legacy Flight Museum at Rexburg, Indiana.

> "I flew in one of the large formations near the back. To watch so many Mustangs thru my windscreen was an amazing experience."
>
> John Bagley

Petie 2nd

N314BG • P-51D-25NA • Les Heikkila

Mustang 44-73140 began serving in the RCAF in 1947. Twenty years later, it was purchased by Burns Byram who named the plane *Tangerine*. The aircraft had various owners and under the ownership of Dennis Bradley crashed in a forced landing in 1982. In 1987, it was rebuilt at Chino, and one year later was painted to represent Lt. Col. John C. Meyer's *Petie 2nd* by owner Doug Arnold. It is currently under the ownership of Les Heikkila.

Blue Nosers have one of the most recognized P-51 Mustang paint schemes from World War II.

Petie 2nd

N5427V • P-51D-25NA • Tony Buechler

Petie 2nd was delivered to USAAF the 19th of February, 1945. It was shipped to the Mediterranean Theater of Operations and saw combat service in the 12th and 15th Air Force at the end of the war. This P-51 was possibly a Tuskegee aircraft, but the exact disposition while overseas is unknown. *Petie 2nd* served in many Air National Guard units until sold as surplus in 1957 to Dale Newton for $755.00. It was owned by Robert Fulton from 1962 until 1984. Rebuilt by Gordon Plaskett, it was sold to Tony Buechler in 1985, the current owner.

The 352nd Fighter Group was comprised of the 328th, 486th, and 487th Fighter Squadrons, all Blue Nosed Mustangs. The 487th was led by Lt. Col. John C. Meyer, in *Petie 3rd*.

Petie 3rd

N51PT • P-51D-20NA • Jeff Pryor

Early in 1945, this aircraft rolled off the assembly line in Ingelwood, California and was shipped to Europe. Although the records indicate no action during World War II, this aircraft actively served in the Air National Guard until 1962. In the late '80s, the plane was restored and painted with the scheme from John C. Meyer's *Petie 3rd*.

After a crash, this Mustang was the subject of a major restoration effort and now sports an olive drab paint scheme.

Polar Bear

N51Z • P-51A-1NA • Jerry Gabe

In 1943, this Mustang, then named *Mines Field*, was delivered to the Army Air Corps, Ladd Field, Arkansas. In 1944 it crashed near Summit, Alaska, killing the pilot. Once wreckage was recovered in 1977, it went through an eight-year restoration in Ohio, returning to flight in 1985. In 2005, the plane entered the Reno Air Races. The next year *Polar Bear* won a Sunday Bronze Victory.

Polar Bear is a rare A model North American P-51. These early Mustangs began with three-bladed props before moving up to a standard four-bladed propeller on all subsequent models of the aircraft.

This Mustang's original Merlin engine was removed to make room for the more powerful Rolls-Royce Griffon, commonly used in the Supermarine Spitfire.

Precious Metal

N6WJ • P-51D-25NA • Ron Buccarelli

Precious Metal, rebuilt to race at the National Championship Air Races in Reno, Nevada, is a highly modified P-51 Mustang. It is the only Mustang in the world powered by the mighty Rolls-Royce Griffon V-12 engine, the bigger brother of the Merlin, the most iconic and successful engine from World War II. *Precious Metal* also contains contra-rotating propellers, completely eliminating torque and P-Factor. Other modifications include clipped wings, turtle deck, and a racing canopy.

Mustang pilots use a lot of right rudder during takeoff to counter the effects of what's called "p-factor," an aerodynamic force causing the airplane to veer left. *Precious Metal's* twin counter-rotating propellers remove all asymmetric thrust.

Princess Elizabeth

N487FS • P-51C-10NT • Jim Beasley

Princess Elizabeth, one of only a few surviving P-51C versions, was acquired in 2006 from Stephen Grey's Fighter Collection. After a seven-year overhaul, Stephen created one of the most "original" Mustangs flying. *Princess Elizabeth* sat for years until the late 1970s, when Pete Regina reassembled and flew her as Don Gentile's 4th Fighter Group "Shangri-La" scheme. In the mid-1980s, Joe Kasparoff purchased her and repainted her as a postwar racer.

Quick Silver's owner says his aircraft's unique black paint scheme represents "the veil of protection that our armed forces give us."

"It was an honor to be part of such an iconic gathering of friends, family, colleagues, and the greatest fighter aircraft of all time."

Bill & Scott Yoak

Quick Silver N51HY • P-51D-30NT • Rancho Linda Vista, LLC.

The silver ring behind the spinner is said to represent the shining halo of a guardian angel. Close inspection of the black paint also reveals tiny sparkling stars.

Quick Silver is the result of a fourteen-year reconstruction program. The project was done by Bill Yoak and was completed just in time for its debut at Oshkosh 2007, where it won Reserve Grand Champion and Gold Wrenches for the reconstruction crew. The paint scheme is a flying celebration of this nation's veterans and those who give the ultimate sacrifice. Scott "Scooter" Yoak flies *Quick Silver*, and it is crewed by his father, Bill Yoak.

Nose art began on aircraft as a way of identifying "friendlies." Over time the practice evolved into an art form that often expressed the individuality of the craft's pilot and crew.

Red Dog XII

N334FS • P-51D-25NA • Duane Doyle

Built in 1944, *Red Dog XII* went to the 8th Air Force in England in 1945, but saw no combat before the war ended. In 1958, it was sold to Guatemala where it served until 1972. Connie Edwards returned her to the U.S. and stored the aircraft until 1999. Its current owner, Mr. Doyle, bought the plane in 1999, still in military configuration. He disassembled the plane, put it through a two-year restoration, and painted it as *Red Dog XII*, as flown by Major Louis Norley of the 4th Fighter Group, 334th Fighter Squadron.

Though *Red Dog XII* came along too late to see combat in WWII, she is nevertheless a great example of the final evolution of P-51D model.

With the markings of the 4th Fighter Group, *Ridge Runner III* featured nose art of a wild hog.

Ridge Runner III   N151DM • P-51D-20NA • Dan Martin

Mustang 44-63769 was shipped to the European Theater during World War II, and then was sold to Sweden. It went back and forth from the U.S. to Latin American countries until purchased by Jack Flarety in 1974. The plane's restoration took three years, from 1974 to 1977. Once completed, Dan Martin raced her for many years at the Reno Air Races. *Ridge Runner III* currently resides in Hollister, California.

Scat VII   N93TF • TF-51D-25NA • Flight Management LLC

Scat VII started her career with the 479th Fighter Group, 434th Fighter Squadron as the personal mount of Robin Olds. Surplused in the early 1950s, she passed though various owners until being acquired by John Dilley of Ft. Wayne Air Service in the late 1980s. The aircraft was highly modified as an unlimited air racer and named *Miss Vendetta*. After an engine failure and resultant crash at Reno, the plane was sold to Jim Shuttleworth and rebuilt as a TF-51. Mr. Shuttleworth put her back in Robin Olds' colors and Robin was subsequently reunited with the plane. Sadly, Jim Shuttleworth lost his life in the plane in 2003. Airpower Unlimited acquired the wreckage in 2005 and once again rebuilt *Scat VII*.

The P-51 features both main gear and a tail wheel which retract to reduce the aircraft's drag.

Section Eight

N2869D • P-51D-25NT • Doug Driscoll

In 1963, Mustang N2869D, was *Bardahl Special* racer #8 and owned by Charles Lyford. Fifteen years later in 1978, the Life Science Church in California acquired the plane, and then in 1981 it was owned by Charles Hall as racer #3. From there, the plane went through different owners. Current owner, Doug Driscoll, purchased *Section Eight* in 1983 and completed restoration in 2006.

The term *Section Eight* has its roots in World War II when the phrase referred to someone who was unfit for military duty, primarily due to mental illness.

The Gathering of Mustangs & Legends

Shangrila

N51VF • P-51D-30NT • Charles Osborne

Major Don Gentile primarily flew his legendary olive drab C model P-51 in combat. Upon completion of his tour in 1944, North American Aviation produced this brand new P-51D for Don in appreciation of his heroic actions. The new D model was painted like Don's original C model with some minor changes. Completely restored to better than new condition, *Shangrila* still flies in tribute to one of this nation's highest scoring aces – Major Don S. Gentile.

Shangrila, with her stylized checkerboard nose also features the nose art of the Eagle Squadrons comprised of American volunteers.

Shangrila
XB-HVL • P-51D-25NA • Humberto Lobo de La Garza

This Mustang crashed on June 7, 1968, but was rebuilt using I.d. 44-72934 by Pioneer Aero Service in June 1991. Doug Arnold of Warbirds of Great Britain Ltd. in the U.K. owned her from 1991 to 1994. The Mustang was named *Shangrila*. Then it was sold to its current owner, moved to Mexico in 1994, and continues to fly as 44-72934 *Shangrila*.

"It has really been an honor to be a P-51 Mustang owner and pilot, but flying in formation at The Gathering of Mustangs and Legends was a dream come true."

Humberto Lobo de la Garza

The exhaust from the right side cylinders are matched on the other side. The P-51 featured a Rolls-Royce Merlin V-12 liquid-cooled engine.

Sizzlin' Liz
N351DM • P-51D-30NA • Dave Marco

Sizzlin' Liz began her career in the Royal Canadian Air Force. Upon being surplused, the plane went through various civilian owners before being purchased by John Marlin in 1973. Marlin rebuilt the plane and flew her in the colors of the prototype P-51D #102. He named the plane *Daydreamer*. David Marco purchased her in 1988 and commissioned Glenn Wegman of Fighter Enterprises to undertake a complete restoration. Upon completion, Marco painted the plane in 4th Fighter Group colors representing Maj. Gerald Montgomery. *Sizzlin' Liz* took home the Grand Champion Award at Oshkosh in 1991.

"Stories from teary-eyed veterans lured to the airport from that familiar overhead sound they had not heard since the war. Emotional stories as they touch the warm cowling — shaking, they tell of all too many friends that died while bombing over enemy lines. Every day more and more friends did not return. And the Mustang appeared — it saved my life."

David Marco

Slender, Tender & Tall

N51DT • CA-18 MK.23 • Tom Blair

In 1950, *Slender, Tender & Tall* became part of the Royal Australian Air Force and was assigned I.D. A68-175. In 1965, she found her way into civilian hands when acquired by Ed Fleming. Then, in 1967 she was shipped to Canada by John Kehler, and in 1971, she adopted the I.D. 44-74950. She returned to the States in 1976 when obtained by John Silberman of Florida, and from this point passed through several owners, until reaching her current owner, Thomas Blair, in 1999.

"I humbly tip my hat to Angela, Lee, and all the other folks that made The Gathering a reality. They orchestrated a seemingly impossible event, an event that was truly magnificent."

Tom Blair

Sparky

N151D • P-51-D-25NA • Steve Seghetti

Built by North American in Inglewood, California in 1944, 44-72777 became the personal mount
of Captain Doc Watson, an ace with five kills. It sold for $1,200.00 to Cavalier Aircraft in 1969
after having served with the Rhode Island and California Air National Guard units. Purchased by
Indonesia in 1969, it returned to the States in 1979. Steve Seghetti acquired the plane in 1984 and
with friends completed the plane's restoration in 1987. It has been a constant participant at the
Reno Air Races since 1994.

Speedball Alice
N64824 • P-51D-30NA • Dan Vance

Speedball Alice was delivered to the RCAF in 1950. In 1976, she came into civilian ownership under Art Vance. Rebuilt in 1982 and named *Million Dollar Baby*, she didn't acquire the name, *Speedball Alice* until 2000. Sadly, in October of 2005, the long time owner of *Speedball Alice* was killed when the Grumman Hellcat he was flying hit power lines in Tennessee. Vance was 64 at the time and ferrying the Planes of Fame aircraft to an Arkansas show. Art's son, Dan Vance, continues to operate *Speedball Alice* as a tribute to his father and the 357th Fighter Group.

A scarcity of original Mustang parts led to the creation of this aircraft's Odegaard Wing, which was mounted on a fuselage modified by restoration guru Gerry Beck.

Sweet and Lovely

N451D • P-51D-25NA • Bob Baker

This airplane was nothing more than a collection of Mustang parts when Bob Baker combined them with a Beck fuselage and an Odegaard wing. Restored in the markings of Lt. Cuthbert A. "Bill" Pattillo's Mustang of the 487th Fighter Squadron, 352nd Fighter Group, *Sweet and Lovely* was displayed at Oshkosh 2004. She featured the 108-gallon paper drop tanks as used in World War II. *Sweet and Lovely* won Grand Champion World War II and Bob won the Gold Wrench award.

Numbers like these on the tail refer to the aircraft's original registration numbers.

Legend Bill Pattillo flew 35 combat missions over Europe in a Blue Nose Mustang he called *Sweet and Lovely*. Later he would fly with the USAF Thunderbirds.

Sweet Revenge

N68JR • P-51D-20NA • Ron & Diane Fagen

Sweet Revenge was delivered to the USAAF, 8th Air Force in 1945 and sold on to the Swedish Air Force in the same year. In 1952, it was sold to the Dominican Republic as FAD 1912, and returned to the U.S. when Brian O'Farrell bought it in 1984. John Sandberg purchased the plane in 1985, and it was restored as *Platinum Plus* Race #28. In 1996, it became *Sweet Revenge* when purchased by Ron and Diane Fagen.

Sweet Revenge represents the 334th Fighter Squadron, one of the three original Eagle Squadrons of the 4th Air Force. The 334th is credited with 395 kills – 210 in the air and 185 on the ground.

"It was great to see such a mix of people, whether it was all the Mustang Legends on hand that flew the Mustang in battle or the little two-year-old boy in the stroller holding his Mustang toy. All people on hand had one thing in common, the love of the P-51 Mustang and the admiration of those who flew these beautiful airplanes in battle."

Ron Fagen

Sweetie Face

N151TP • P-51D-25NA • Tom Patten

Mustang S/N44-73543 was exported from the U.S. in 1945, perhaps for Europe though the records are incomplete. In July of 1945, she returned to the U.S. From 1946 to 1958, it served in the U.S., and then in Indonesia until 1978. The aircraft was shipped to the U.K. where she saw several owners until she was purchased by an American group in 1985 and restored. Tom Patten bought the plane in 1998, naming it *Sweetie Face*. The name was purloined from Lt. Heyer, who flew the original *Sweetie Face* with the 487th Fighter Squadron of the 352nd Fighter Group.

A classic example of the "Blue Nosed Bastards from Bodney," the 352th Fighter Group.

Sweetie Face was flown by Lt. Sheldon Heyer, who flew as wingman for the leader of the 352nd Fighter Group.

Twilight Tear was named by her pilot Lt. Huberet "Bill" Davis after a favorite race horse. She was assigned to Duxford and painted with the markings of the 83rd Fighter Squadron. Ironically, after duties in several other countries after the war, this Mustang now resides in Duxford where it started off more than six decades ago.

Twilight Tear   G-CBNM • P-51D-20NA • Patina, Ltd.

Twilight Tear was delivered to the 78th Fighter Group in 1944 and was the mount of Lt. Hubert "Bill" Davis who named her *Twilight Tear*. By the war's end, Hubert was credited with four confirmed aerial kills. By 1949, the aircraft was exported to the Royal Swedish Air Force and then to Israel. In 1978, Colonel Itzahi acquired, reassembled, and restored the aircraft. *Twilight Tear* came full circle and returned to Duxford, the same airfield she left some sixty years ago. She is now operated by the Fighter Collection at the Imperial War Museum, Duxford.

> "The Gathering was a great event, a tribute to the great people who had the courage to organize it and the remaining wonderful veterans who flew and fought in these iconic aircraft. It was great to meet old friends and new, and I shall always treasure the memory of my 'splashdown' in a Columbus thunderstorm pre-opening night!"
>
> **Stephen Grey**

Voodoo

N551VC • P-51D-25NA • Bob Button

Voodoo was delivered to the Royal Canadian Air Force as 9289 and served from 1951 to 1959. In 1962 it crashed, suffering major damage. The plane passed through various owners during the years of 1966 to 1975 and in 1977, crashed on takeoff under the ownership of William Veatch. William Spears rebuilt the plane and flew it as *Pegasus*. Bob and Christine Button purchased the plane in 1994 and raced it as *Voodoo Chile* #55 N6526D, currently *Voodoo* #5 N551VC.

Voodoo is now highly modified and makes her living at the National Air Races in Reno, Nevada.

This P-51D Mustang is commemorative of Lt. Calvert L. Williams, whose name is on the side, along with four iron cross victory marks. The red and yellow checkerboard pattern on the nose represents the 357th Fighter Group, who were nicknamed "The Yoxford Boys."

Wee Willy II

N7715C • P-51D-25NT • Steve Hinton

In 1967, the plane now known as *Wee Willie II* was flown as race #5 *Miss RJ* and piloted by Chuck Hall. In 1971, it became the highly modified *Roto Finish Special*. In 1975, the aircraft was painted bright red and named *Red Baron*. A team of engineers installed a Rolls-Royce Griffon engine and three-blade contra – rotating props from a British Shackleton bomber. In 1979, the *Red Baron* achieved the world piston engine speed record at 499.08 mph. Sadly, she crashed the same year during a race at Reno, severely injuring pilot Steve Hinton. In 1985, Steve Hinton and Fighter Rebuilders, with the assistance of various wrecked P-51s, restored her as a stock P-51D in the 357th Fighter Group colors of *Wee Willie II*.

"Our flight of six originated from Texas. No one wanted to miss the rare opportunity to fly in a large formation of P-51s; something that had not been done since the 40s."

Steve Hinton

Worry Bird is a stock P-51 Mustang sent to England to join the 8th Air Force, the largest deployed combat Army Air Forces in numbers of personnel, aircraft, and equipment.

Worry Bird

N951M • P-51D-25NA • Mike George

On April 13, 1945, *Worry Bird* left the United States for the 8th Air Force, European Theater of Operations. It returned to the U.S. on July 18th of the same year. In 1948, *Worry Bird* was redesigned as an F-51D and assigned to the 188th Fighter Squadron of the Air National Guard at Kirtland Air Force Base. In January 1954 it was assigned to the 165th Fighter Bomber Squadron of the Kentucky Air National Guard. In 1958, it was dropped from the United States Air Force inventory and sold for $957.95.

Worry Bird flew with the 8th Air Force stationed at High Wycombe Airdrome in England during the war. She flew bomber support for missions into Northern Europe. The 8th Air Force is now part of the Air Force Global Strike Command and operates the B-2 and B-52 bombers.

The NACA logo on the vertical stabilizer stands for the National Advisory Committee for Aeronautics, which made important contributions to the development and production of military aircraft that saw service during the war.

NACA 127

N51YZ • P-51D-25NT • Bill Allmon

Built in 1945, Mustang 44-84900 was acquired by the National Advisory Committee for Aeronautics (NACA) for the expressed purpose of verifying aerodynamic data being produced by wind tunnels. It was assigned the number *NACA 127* and was utilized from 1945 to 1952. Raised panels were installed mid-chord onto which the NACA engineers placed models of airfoils and airframes which were tested in transonic wing flow. After a four year restoration, *NACA 127* was the 1998 Oshkosh Warbird Grand Champion.

The NACA was a federal agency created to promote aeronautical research.

On October 1, 1958 the agency was dissolved and transferred to the National Aeronautics and Space Administration (NASA).

Photos: Courtesy Curtis Fowles, Mustangs Mustangs

44-63889

N4034S • P-51D-20NA • John Anderson

44-63889 was assigned to the 325th Fighter Group (the "Checkertail Clan"), 318th Fighter Squadron. It was #60 and assigned to Lt. Albert S. Hall. After the war, the aircraft was returned to the U.S. and had a long post-war service, which included Strategic Air Command service in New Mexico, New Hampshire, and California; Air Defense Command service in New York, Wisconsin, and Minnesota; and, finally, the Air National Guard service in Maryland. The aircraft was dropped from inventory in 1958 following commercial sale. *44-63889* was also formerly the *Black Mustang* owned by Gary McCann of Canada. In 2002, it was purchased by its current owner, John Anderson, and it has been undergoing work since then.

44-73420

N7722C • P-51D-25NA • Jack Croul

Mustang *44-73420* was shipped to Italy joining the 15th Air Force but never made it into combat before the war's end. Returning stateside, it was assigned to several Air National Guard units. Eventually released and sold by the United States Air Force in 1958 for $895.00, *44-73420* began civilian life with several owners, including Rob Satterfield who campaigned it as *Miss Torque*. After Rob's death, it was sold to the Alpine Fighter Collection in Wanaka, New Zealand where it flew as one of the Breitling Fighters before being acquired by Jack Croul in June 2003.

44-73420 is the serial number of this P-51, produced toward the end of World War II. Much of this cockpit has been restored to original condition. The yellow line was used to distinguish primary flight instruments from system instruments.

> "I met a person with knowledge of the whereabouts of a rare windscreen for the G. Later, I obtained this windscreen. This was only made possible by my attending The Gathering of Mustangs and Legends."
>
> **John Morgan**

Margie Hart   XP-51G • John Morgan

Margie Hart is a lightweight, XP-51G Mustang. In 1943, the British wanted the Mustang reduced in weight to the standards of the Spitfire, and the result was a proof-of-concept aircraft, the best combination of propeller and airframe. The G had a Rolls-Royce Merlin 14.SM of 2,200 horsepower and a North American Aviation airframe. Thinner wings, smaller landing gear wheels, and many other firsts on an aircraft lightened the weight to 5, 749 pounds empty. At 46,000 feet, it was the highest flying Mustang and the fastest of the lightweight Mustangs at 498 mph.

Margie Hart was the only XP-51G present at The Gathering. Since the plane was in the restoration process, *Margie Hart* was trucked in from California and displayed as a static aircraft. The presence of this unique Mustang gave many attendees the opportunity to compare the D model to the experimental G model.

The Gathering helped owner John Morgan with his restoration project. He recalls, "I met a person with knowledge of the whereabouts of a rare windscreen for the G. Later, I obtained this windscreen. This was only made possible by my attending The Gathering of Mustangs and Legends."

THE LEGENDS

Most of the 51 Legends had simply been living their lives when the phone call came. "You are among the men and women who have been chosen. Would you come to the Gathering of Mustangs and Legends?"

Army Air Corps Ace Lt. Leedom "Kirk" John said, "To bring us old World War II pilots together was a good idea!"

P-51 fighter pilot Lt. Colonel Robert J. Frisch said,

"When I returned from overseas, so did everyone else so there was no great recognition of what had been accomplished." He would be honored to be acknowledged at The Gathering of Mustangs and Legends.

From autograph signings to photo shoots, the Legends seemed surprised over the giant outpouring of people interested in hearing their stories.

INTRODUCTION

With the remarkable success of The Gathering in Kissimmee, Florida in 1999, there was no reason to wonder if there would be interest in recreating the event on a much larger scale. Thousands of people had turned up with little or no publicity to alert them just to have a chance to hear stories from the men who flew the P-51 in the war, and, of course, to see the magnificent warbirds themselves. It could all be done again, except this time on a world scale. So began the planning for The Gathering of Mustangs and Legends 2007.

Preparation for such an event was onerous, demanding, and at times approached grueling. A venue had to be chosen, a venue that could accommodate as many as 200,000 people. The year 2007 was also the 60th anniversary of the United States Air Force, and they expressed an extreme interest in participating in this new gathering. Adding their celebration meant offering up the precision demonstration team, the world famous Thunderbirds, as well as performing Heritage Flights, where vintage aircraft flying alongside the newest USAF hardware. Now the venue not only needed to accommodate a crowd, it needed to have a runway long enough to accommodate the F-15, F-16, and F-22 Raptor. All of this was laid on top of searching the map for all of the airworthy P-51 Mustangs that could come. And how do you select and then find the Legends that designed, flew, and maintained these airplanes more than sixty years ago?

WHY 51 LEGENDS?

The first decision made was to commit to searching out the best of the best, the men and women who are as important to the history of the P-51 as the airplane was to them. That meant finding pilots, Mustang aces (if not double and triple aces), Tuskegee Airmen, and WASPs, as well as people who spent selfless hours turning the wrenches so the aircraft could fight again another day. In the end, 51 Legends were selected — 51 matching the North American Mustang's number — representing the family of people who made significant contributions in making the P-51 the most important airplane of World War II and the most iconic warbird the world has even known.

PILOTS/ACES

They served their country by sitting for hours in small, freezing cold cockpits, matching speeds with a flight of lumbering bombers. There would eventually be swarms of Luftwaffe, clouds of anti-aircraft fire, and, of course, dog fights to deal with. Some of these pilots made the ultimate sacrifice, others became prisoners of war. A lucky few became aces, with at least five airborne kills to their credit. They were youngsters really, young men and women who learned to fly when their country needed them the most. Foremost was the duty at hand, and they did it selflessly in the dark and in the daylight, many never knowing if they'd just finished their last meal. Eventually their sacrifices would turn the tide of the war.

CREWMEN

You owe Charles Edward Taylor a debt of gratitude, even though you likely do not recognize the name. He was the mechanical genius behind the Wright brothers, building their aircraft engines and maintaining their fragile aircraft so that mankind could cross the threshold of powered flight for the very first time on December 3, 1903. In much the same way as Charles Edward Taylor surely made the accomplishments at Kill Devil Hills possible, so did the crewmen assigned to keeping the P-51 Mustang in service. They spent long hours dedicated to getting their birds in the air again, dealing with bullet holes, flack damage, blown engines, and countless other gremlins conspiring to wash out the next mission. Often these men were shortchanged the acknowledgement and appreciation for the long hours and numerous sacrifices they made in the name of the war effort. These crewmen received a special salute at The Gathering of Mustangs and Legends in recognition of their roles that uniquely enabled the pilots and P-51s to do their jobs.

DESIGNERS/BUILDERS

It would be difficult to overstate the contribution North American Aircraft made in establishing air superiority in Europe. They had promised the British they could design and fly a whole new pursuit aircraft in just 120 days…and they did. They called it the P-51 Mustang.

The aircraft would be state-of-the-art, taking advantage of the latest innovations both in design and application. When it was determined the aircraft was weak at fighting at high altitudes, designers had the builders install a whole new engine, the supercharged Rolls-Royce Merlin. That single change transformed the North American P-51 into the most capable air-to-air combat aircraft in either theater of war.

Though the first models of the Mustang were markedly different than the last, the P-51 was the first fighter that could escort Allied bombers all the way to the target and back again. That fact, added to the Mustang's ability to engage the enemy at speeds in excess of 400 mph, then nimbly fight all the way to 40,000 feet, was the beginning of the end for the Luftwaffe.

DUDLEY AMOSS

Dudley Moore Amoss was born on July 7, 1922 in Baltimore, Maryland. After enlisting in 1942, he was assigned to the 38th Fighter Squadron of the 55th Fighter Group, starting out as a Staff Sergeant and then given the non-commissioned rank of Flight Officer.

His first contributions came in September 1944 when Amoss destroyed an unidentified enemy plane and shared in the destruction of a Junkers JU-52/3M on the ground. On his 59th and final mission in March 1945, Amoss was taking one final strafing pass across an airfield when he was hit by ground fire in the radiator. As he was limping back to Allied territory, he came upon three FW-190s returning from a mission. Flying low, Amoss was able to pull in behind the leader and hit him as he turned, forcing him to clip the trees and crash. Amoss then turned on the second and, just like the first, caused the FW-190 to clip the trees and go down. As the third German pilot tried in vain to turn away, Amoss turned with him, shot him down and, that quickly, Amoss was an ace.

PURSUIT TO DEFEND

55th Fighter Group

CLARENCE E. "BUD" ANDERSON

Bud Anderson learned to fly at the age of 19, then joined the U.S. Army Aviation Cadet program and received his wings in September 1942. He joined the 357th Fighter Group which was sent to England in November 1943 and became the first P-51 Mustang unit in the 8th Air Force. Colonel Anderson served two tours of combat in Europe, flew 116 combat missions (480 hours), and shot down 16 1/4 enemy aircraft in aerial combat. He also destroyed another enemy aircraft on the ground and was the leading ace in the 363rd Fighter Squadron. Bud Anderson has logged over 8,000 hours and flown 130 different types of aircraft. As a triple ace, Colonel Anderson has been decorated 26 times, including two Legion Merits, five Distinguished Flying Crosses, the Bronze Star, 16 Air Medals, the French Legion of Honor, and the French Croix de guerre, as well as many campaign and service ribbons. He remains an active pilot, maintaining a Flight Instructor rating, and occasionally flies a P-51. He lectures on his flying experiences and has consulted on computer combat simulation games.

357th Fighter Group

"To attend a Gathering that showcased many restored, flyable Mustangs and a selection of folks that flew and supported them was beyond awesome!"

Bud Anderson is s triple ace who flew with the 357th Fighter Group out of Leiston Field, U.K.

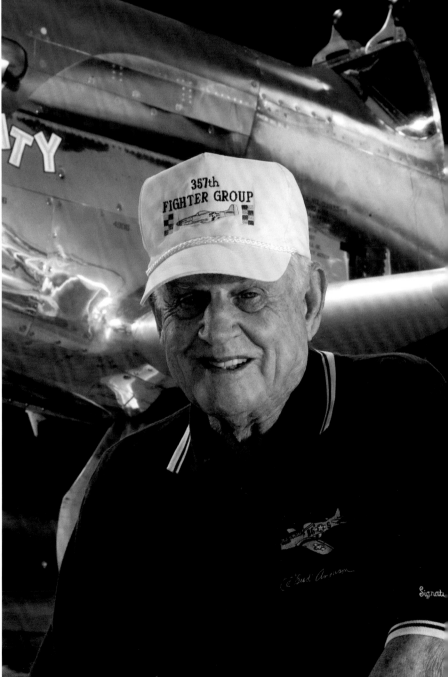

In December 1942, Lee Archer reported to Tuskegee Army Airfield as an Aviation Cadet, where he graduated at the head of his class on July 28, 1943. Archer was promoted to 2nd Lieutenant and then assigned to the 332nd Fighter Group, receiving advanced training before his group was transferred to Italy in January 1944. His first few months in Italy, Archer flew P-39s in ground support and patrol missions. The 332nd later received P-47 Thunderbolts and, finally, P-51 Mustangs. In the P-51, Archer scored a total of five kills — three on one engagement on October 12, 1944. He flew a total of 169 missions and also destroyed six aircraft on the ground.

Archer was awarded the Distinguished Flying Cross, the Air Medal with 18 Clusters, the Distinguished Unit Citation, and many other service medals. He retired from the Air Force in 1971 and is the only ace of the famed Tuskegee Airmen.

332nd Fighter Group

Lee Archer, in a heated battle of German-occupied Hungary, shot down three BF-109s. He is the only ace among the Tuskegee Airmen.

ERNEST E. BANKEY

Ernest Bankey signed up with the Army Air Corps at Fort Hayes in Columbus, Ohio on April 1, 1941. He earned his wings with class 43-G at Williams Air Force Base in Arizona and shipped out to the European Theater. In two tours of duty, Bankey compiled over 100 sorties and 500 combat hours. Mission reports credit him with 10 air destroyed, one probable, five ground destroyed, and five enemy aircraft damaged. He was awarded the Distinguished Service Cross for shooting

Bankey, a triple ace, shot down five German airplanes in one day during the Battle of the Bulge.

8th Air Force

down five aircraft on one mission during the Battle of the Bulge on December 27, 1944 when the group was awarded the Distinguished Unit Citation. Additional awards include the Silver Star, Distinguished Flying Cross with Clusters, Air Medal with Nine Clusters, and French Croix de guerre with Palm.

In 1968, Colonel Ernest Bankey retired from the United States Air Force at Strategic Air Command Headquarters, Nebraska. He moved his family to California and joined the Jet Propulsion Laboratories in Pasadena where he worked on deep-space projects, some of which, remarkably, fly on the outer edges of our solar system still today.

BETTY BLAKE

Betty Blake was one of the original Women Air Force Service Pilots (WASP) to serve the United States during World War II. From Honolulu, Blake trained in a J3, earning free flight time by working at a local airport and later flying tourists around the islands in open cockpit planes.

She married an ensign stationed aboard the battleship California that was later sunk at Pearl Harbor. The two returned to the states where she served in the Ferry Command, operating everything from L-5s to B-17s and B-24s. Her favorite plane was the P-51, a number of which she ferried to Alaska for Russian pilots, who flew them to Russia to fight against the Germans.

Her time now is spent giving talks at clubs for the Air Force and in schools. She also enjoys writing articles and fiction and having fun with her four dogs and horses.

WASP
Women Air Force Service Pilots

As a WASP, Betty Blake ferried B-17s,
P-51s, P-38s across the country.
She learned to fly at the age of 14.

JAMES BROOKS

A native of Roanoke, Virginia, James L. Brooks joined the Air Force in 1942. In early 1944, he joined the 31st Fighter Group in Italy and the group then exchanged their Spitfires for P-51 Mustangs. They provided long range escort for heavy bombers deep into Europe and the Balkan Islands.

Brooks recorded his first victory over Ploesti, Romania in April 1944. While on a special mission from Russia to Lvov, Poland, Brooks led the 307th Fighter Squadron on an engagement with 40 JU-87 Stuka dive bombers. 27 of the 40 enemy aircraft were destroyed and the 31st received its second Unit Citation. Brooks also received the Silver Star. He ended his tour with 280 combat hours, 13 confirmed kills, and three damaged aircraft in the air, mostly ME-109s.

His decorations include the Silver Star, the Distinguished Flying Cross with one Oak Leaf Cluster, the Air Medal with 20 Oak Leaf Clusters, and the Unit Citation with one Oak Leaf Cluster.

31st Fighter Group

James Brooks started his military career with the 52nd Fighter Squadron tasked with protecting the Panama Canal flying P-39s and P-40s.

ROSCOE BROWN

332nd Fighter Group

Dr. Roscoe C. Brown, Jr. served as squadron commander of the 100th Fighter Squadron of the 332nd Fighter Group – the famed Tuskegee Airmen.

Brown flew his first combat mission escorting B-24 bombers over the Ploesti oil fields in Romania in August 1944. In all, Brown completed 68 combat missions in the P-51 Mustang, escorting bombers over Germany, Austria, and the Balkan Islands and conducting low altitude strafing missions over

enemy airfields and rail yards. The highlight of his combat career came when he was the first 15th Air Force fighter pilot to shoot down a German ME-262 jet fighter. During that same mission, the 332nd Fighter Group was selected to receive the highest honor given to a combat unit, the Presidential Unit Citation.

The 332nd Fighter Group's successful combat record, including downing 111 enemy aircraft and damaging another 150 on the ground, was a principal factor in President Truman's decision to integrate the armed forces in 1948. For his achievements in combat, Brown was awarded the Distinguished Flying Cross and the Air Medal with eight Oak Leaf Clusters.

Roscoe Brown is one of only 15 pilots from World War II who shot down the world's first jet fighter, the ME-262.

"I was so proud the Red Tails were represented."

FREDERICK "TED" BULLOCK

Bullock was a member of the 52nd Fighter Group, 4th Fighter Squadron and was close friends with fellow fighter and later renowned test pilot Bob Hoover. Bullock first flew the Spitfire Mark V in North Africa before his unit transitioned first to the P-51B and later the P-51D. During his combat service in North Africa, Sicily, Corsica, and Italy, he flew a total of 70 missions including fighter cover for B-17s and B-24s during the historic Ploesti oil field raids. He shot down three enemy fighters, two ME-109s, and an Italian aircraft in German markings flown by the Romanian Air Force.

From the late 1940s through the early 1970s, Bullock flew all of the first generation jets, from the P-80 to the super sonic F-100. Before retiring, he was awarded the Legion of Merit, Distinguished Flying Cross, Air Medal, and many other service decorations.

One of his final assignments before retiring was as Commander of Wheeler Air Force Base in Hawaii, where World War II began nearly 30 years earlier with the attack of Pearl Harbor.

52nd Fighter Group

Ted Bullock began his aviation career flying the Spitfire Mark V in North Africa until he transitioned to the P-51B and ultimately the P-51D.

BILL CREECH

Bill Creech was a Depression-era boy who entered World War II enticed by the excitement of flight. He entered as a fighter pilot in the United States Army Air Corps and left a man with heroic stories to be published in his memoir.

In 1942, Bill Creech joined the United States Army Air Force, and in China, India, and Burma he flew P-51As and P-51Bs in combat. He was also a member of the Fighter Squadron, 528th Dragonflys, which received the Presidential Unit Citation for extraordinary heroism for their actions in the Burma Offensive.

Serving in the brutal jungles of Burma Colonel Creech flew 60 missions against Japanese military targets as a Dragonfly. Colonel Creech was shot down twice and was forced to survive in the jungle. After retiring from the Air Force, he continued flying and is a licensed Airframe and Powerplant Mechanic.

Creech wrote a book about his war-time flying called *The 3rd Greatest Fighter Pilot*.

"Well, I told my story about having to pee so bad on one flight that I totally filled the relief tube and it was plugged up!!! My description of flying the airplane home and landing while holding a relief tube filled with pee (and not spilling any) had them in stitches."

8th Air Force

354th Fighter Group

After flight training, Dahlberg was assigned to the 9th Air Force, 354th Fighter Group. On his fourth mission, Dahlberg recorded his first kill against an ME-109 over Chartes, France. In August, he would see his first big action when just eight P-51s tangled with some 80 German planes. Dahlberg had shot down four planes and was lining up on the fifth when he heard 20 mm shells hitting his aircraft. He banked into a cloud and bailed out.

The very next month, four more German planes would fall to Dahlberg's guns when 10 P-51s took on 40 FW-190s. 16 German fighters were lost compared to just two Mustangs. In late 1944, he scored two victories on December 1st then scored his final victories of the war on December 19th, shooting down four German aircraft.

During the Battle of the Bulge, Dahlberg was shot down a second time during a ground attack mission the day after Christmas. On Valentine's Day 1945, Dahlberg was shot down a third time and spent the remainder of the war in Luft Stalag #7.

When Dahlberg was drafted in 1941, he wanted to be a cook. Eventually he became an air cadet where one of the instructors was none other than the future Senator Barry Goldwater.

Barrie Davis was commissioned and received his wings in Dothan, Alabama in August 1943.

In May 1944, he was ordered to join the 325th Fighter Group, the "Checkertails," flying Thunderbolts. After seven missions, the 325th was equipped with P-51 Mustangs, which they flew out of the Soviet Union on D-Day, June 6, 1944.

In November 1944, Davis ended his tour as a flight leader, credited with six air victories and six aircraft and 12 locomotives destroyed on the ground. After 70 missions, his decorations include the Silver Star, the Air Medal with 13 Oak Leaf Clusters, and the Purple Heart, which he earned while flying a mission from the Soviet Union. His plane was so badly damaged, it was left at a Ukraine base.

Davis remained in the Air Corps Reserve until 1949, when he joined the North Carolina Army National Guard, an assignment that started as a one-year engagement but he would keep for 27 years.

Davis was a college student in 1941 but dropped out to join the war effort. He would end up becoming an ace flying the P-51.

325th Fighter Group

CLYDE B. EAST

Born in Pittsylvania County, Virginia on July 19, 1921, Clyde Bennett East was the fifth of nine children. At 19, he was admitted to pilot training and his first assignment took him to Europe. East flew interdiction missions in the P-51A Mustang, attacking ground targets in France, Belgium, and Holland.

During the D-Day invasion of Normandy, East and his wingman stumbled upon several FW-190s landing and promptly dispatched them with their .50 caliber machine guns, claiming the first aerial victories of the invasion. Later that fall, East fought against a German counter-offensive in what is now known as the Battle of the Bulge. Becoming a confirmed ace in March 1945, East would go on to claim a total of 13 aerial kills against the German Luftwaffe in World War II.

East was one of the most decorated fighter pilots during World War II, receiving the Silver Star, Distinguished Flying Cross, and Air Medal with 36 Oak Leaf Clusters. In 1955, *The Guinness Book of World Records* listed him as having the highest number of repeat awards of combat medals.

9th Air Force

Clyde East flew 200 combat missions in Europe with 14 confirmed kills. He later served in Korea, flying 100 missions in RF-51s and RF-80s.

VIVIAN EDDY

After Pearl Harbor, the U.S. military realized an extreme pilot shortage and experimented in training civilian women pilots in military aircraft in order to release men for active duty. The plan was the impetus for the WASPs, Women Air Force Service Pilots. By 1944, WASP Vivian Cadman Eddy turned 23 and was already qualified to fly 17 different models of airplanes. After 500 hours she was chosen to train in fighter planes, the P-47, P-39, P-40, and the hottest military fighter plane of that time, the P-51 Mustang.

On December 20, 1944, Eddy's military service reached a halt. A bill to militarize the WASPs was defeated in congress. All the women were to return home at their own expense. 34 years passed before the WASPs were recognized for their contribution to the war effort. In 1978, Congress enacted a law making them veterans.

**Howard Eddy
talking about his WASP wife, Vivian Eddy:**

"As a career Naval Aviator, I'd flown the F4F and F6F planes but had to admit she flew hotter airplanes than I did!"

WASP
Women Air Force Service Pilots

Vivian Eddy had a pilot's license well before she had a driver's license. As a WASP she crisscrossed the country in warbirds.

FRED FEHSENFELD

On his 18th birthday, Fred Fehsenfeld enlisted in the U.S. Army Air Corps and, after training at several bases in Texas, was assigned to the 354th Pioneer Mustang Fighter Group in France. But the day he and the rest of the group arrived, the 354th lost their P-51s and the group flew P-47Ds. The group flew strafing and dive-bomb missions in support of General Patton's 3rd Army.

In February 1945, the P-47s at the 354th were replaced by P-51Ds and the group's air kills increased substantially. Fehsenfeld shot down three FW-190s and one JU-188, as well as three additional FW-190s on the ground. He was awarded the Air Medal with three Silver Clusters and the Silver Star.

He also led his squadron on the last official flight in the European Theater of Operations, barrel-rolling over an Austrian prisoner of war camp to let his fellow pilots know the war in Europe had ended.

On the way back from his mission, Fehsenfeld discovered a squadron of 70 FW-190s and escorted them to the Munich Airdrome, where he accepted the German squadron leader's surrender.

354th Fighter Group

Fehsenfeld enlisted in the U.S. Army Air Corps on his 18th birthday. He would ship off to Texas for flight training.

"Most everyone who flew P-51s had a love affair."

ARTHUR FIEDLER

Fiedler, who was originally assigned as a P-47 instructor at Dover, Delaware, was sent overseas in April 1943 and joined the 317th Fighter Squadron of the 325th Fighter Group of Lesina, Italy. He began flying the P-51C in June 1943 and claimed a probable kill on June 24th. Four days later he bounced two ME-109s.

Fiedler took pictures of the burning wreckage to confirm his victory. As he started to his climb to altitude, he was startled by another ME-109 crossing directly in front of him. Fiedler racked into a vertical bank and scored several hits before his guns jammed. He suddenly found himself sliding into formation with the ME-109. He knew if he turned away he would be a good target so he decided to fire his .45 automatic at his enemy even though he was only 40 feet away! As Fiedler drew his gun, the German bailed out. He took pictures of this also to confirm his victory. In July, he downed two more ME-109s and a FW-190.

Fiedler flew a total of 66 combat missions in World War II.

> "To think that I would be able to see them, touch them, and see formations of them flying was almost too much to hope for. And then I was there! To see a reincarnation of what had been a daily part of my life some 63 years earlier was almost like having another 'Impossible Dream' come true."

325th Fighter Group

Fiedler enlisted in 1942 and got married in 1943. When he left her behind to fulfill a combat role in Europe, he wisely named his airplane after his new wife, Helen.

WILLIAM FOARD

357th Fighter Group

William Foard was born in 1924 in East Orange, New Jersey. He grew up in Wilmington, North Carolina and Marion, South Carolina. In February 1943, Foard entered the U.S. Army Air Corps, attending basic training at Miami Beach, Florida.

After several assignments at airfields across the South, Foard earned his wings and commission as a 2nd Lieutenant in May 1944. He then received orders to join the 357th Fighter Group, 8th Air Force, in Leiston, England, where he flew 23 combat missions in the P-51 Mustang.

From there, Foard transferred to a voluntary Fighter Group being formed to fly in the Pacific and was eventually assigned to the 339th Fighter Group at Fowlmere. He was then transferred back to the U.S., arriving after V-J Day.

Foard finished his active duty career at Drew Field, Tampa, Florida, where he was discharged in December 1945. He remained active in the Air Force Reserve until June 1972.

> "The icing on the cake was meeting little kids with their bright and shining faces being excited about getting to talk to who they thought was a 'famous P-51 pilot' and having their picture taken with me. That'll puff up any old fogey."

William Foard took part in main escort raids and fighter actions during the final phase of the air war until the end of hostilities.

ROBERT J. FRISCH

Bob Frisch was born in 1924 and entered the Army Air Corps flying school in 1943. He graduated in April 1944 and was assigned to the 339th Fighter Group in October 1944.

During World War II, Frisch flew 61 missions and destroyed six enemy aircraft on the ground and damaged one in the air.

He remained in the Air Force for 27 years and flew the P-40, F-51, F-86, F-89, and F-102 aircraft. He also delivered the first F-106 to the Air Force in 1959. He retired from service in December 1969.

After the military, Frisch entered the real estate business, becoming a broker and eventually a partner in the largest real estate firm in Spokane, Washington. He retired from selling real estate in 1995 and became a real estate developer. He remains active in that business today.

339th Fighter Group

Lieutenant Robert J. Frisch destroyed six enemy aircraft during ground strafing runs.

BILL GETZ

Bill Getz enjoyed a long and distinguished career as an Air Force pilot and officer.

After his combat tour in the 491st Bomb Group ended, he volunteered to extend his combat tour and become a P-51 Mustang pilot. He was one of the first multi-role pilots in the 8th Air Force…perhaps before multi-role was even a defined term.

After serving as aircraft commander of the B-24 Phantom Brigade, where he and his crew completed their 31 combat missions in just 69 days, Getz was the youngest ex-bomber pilot P-51 scout in the 8th Air Force. He was also its youngest four-engine bomber crew commander and youngest flight leader.

He completed two combat tours and was promoted to Captain before he could legally drink or vote. He flew his last combat mission the day after his 21st birthday.

He was awarded two Distinguished Flying Crosses, seven Air Medals, a Presidential Unit Citation, and the European Theater Ribbon with six combat stars.

8th Air Force

"I could literally feel the excitement, if only briefly, of those moments on the tarmac at Steeple Morden Airfield in England, home of the 355th Fighter Group and my own unit, the Second Air Division Scouting Force, P-51 drivers all. I was there once again with Johnny Brooks, Bob Whitlow, "Gooney Bird" Whalen, and so many others, all gone. For the moment, I was young again."

Bill Getz flew a complete tour of duty in B-24s over Europe before transitioning into P-51 Mustangs, where he flew another 175 combat hours.

ROBERT GREEN

78th Fighter Group

After completing just nine weeks of Operational Training piloting P-47s in Atchim, England, Robert Green was assigned to the 78th Fighter Group, 83rd Fighter Squadron. He flew 46 combat missions in P-47s and another 48 in the P-51 Mustang.

In July of 1945, he served in the Air Force Reserve Unit at Long Beach Municipal Airport, California as an instructor and test pilot, flying AT-6s, C-45s, and B-26s. After this, in 1950 he was recalled to active duty with the 452nd Bomb Wing staff, as Air Control Maintenance Officer, flying B-26 Attack Bombers, and in November of 1950 he was deployed to SEA, Japan. This same year, he was moved to Korea as the 452nd Wing Group Material Officer and a pilot, flying B-26s in 20 combat missions.

In 1951, Green was transferred into the 49th Fighter Wing at K-2 as Group Material Officer, flying F-80s, T-32s, and F-84s, for ten combat missions. He returned to the United States in 1953 and was assigned to Lockheed Air Force Plant, Burbank, California as a test pilot for T-33s.

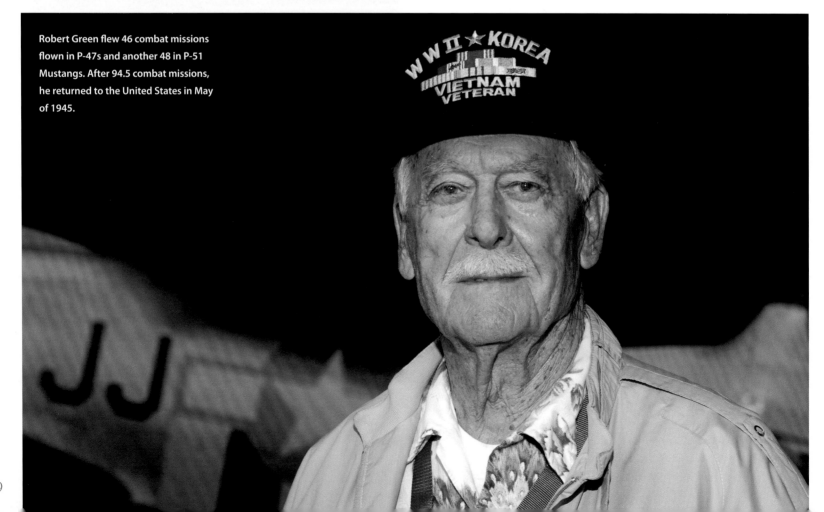

Robert Green flew 46 combat missions flown in P-47s and another 48 in P-51 Mustangs. After 94.5 combat missions, he returned to the United States in May of 1945.

CLAYTON KELLY GROSS

354th Fighter Group

Dr. Clayton Kelly Gross was sent to the European Theater flying the P-47 Thunderbolt with the 354th Fighter Group until 1944 when he transitioned into the P-51 Mustang (his aircraft dubbed *Live Bait*). That year he was credited with five aerial victories over German BF-109 fighters, promptly achieving his status as an ace. However, in 1945, he successfully shot down a German ME-262 jet fighter. The Air Force's official roster of aerial victories does not list this as a kill, but it was recognized during the war as well as the by the American Fighter Aces Association. The ME-262 pilot was injured but managed to bail out, and in 1995 Gross was able to finally meet the pilot, Kurt Lobgesong. Because of Lobgesong's injuries, he was unable to fly in combat again, yet told Gross "you saved my life."

For his actions during the war, Gross received the Silver Star, Distinguished Flying Cross, Air Medal, and Distinguished Unit Citation. He was discharged from the Army Air Corps as a Captain in September of 1945.

In 1944 Gross was credited with five aerial victories over German BF-109 fighters, and in 1945 he successfully shot down a German ME-262 jet fighter.

ROBERT W. GRUENHAGEN

Colonel Robert W. Gruenhagen joined the Montana Air National Guard on December 5, 1947. After graduation from high school in 1949, he attended the Air Force airplane and engine mechanic course at Sheppard AFB, Texas.

In August 1950, Colonel Gruenhagen was employed as an Air Technician with the Montana Air National Guard with duties as a crew chief on F-51 aircraft. In March 1951, he was called to active duty with the 186th Fighter Squadron and served at stateside bases with SAC and TAC and overseas with the Icelandic Defense Force. His duties included assignments as flight chief, line chief, and quality control inspector.

Gruenhagen continued a long and active career in the military working on numerous aircraft. In 1978, Colonel Gruenhagen was selected as the Technician Chief of Maintenance. His military duty as the Deputy Commander for Maintenance was assigned on July 12, 1983. He served in this assignment until his retirement in 1987.

> "The chance to participate as a 'Legend' was an honor that resulted in yet another life-changing event influenced by that wonderful machine, the P-51 Mustang."

Colonel Gruenhagen worked as an Air Technician with the Montana Air National Guard with duties as a crew chief on P-51 aircraft.

James Herbert flew 14 combat missions in P-38s and 43 in P-51s.

Herbert arrived at the 77th Fighter Squadron a few days after the D-Day invasion. He considers himself lucky to have been assigned to Captain Jim "Slick" Morris's flight flying P-38s. From Morris, Herbert adopted the much appreciated practice of turning around on a journey home to escort a crippled bomber calling for help.

Herbert recalls one such mission in his P-51. He was escorting one bomber back when another called for help. The wounded ship's crew was throwing everything out of their plane to make it lighter. Herbert convinced them to throw out their radio too, and if he hadn't, they may not have even made it to their emergency landing field on the English coast. Herbert stayed with them for half an hour after they ditched and called for "Dumbo." He then buzzed them, did a slow roll, and headed for home. He ran into the crew a few days following in a London pub, and he spent no money on drinks that evening.

> "It was very satisfying and amazing to see the interest of so many young people. I have never signed so many programs, pictures, jackets, caps, T-shirts, and one automobile hood in my life!"

VICTORY BY VALOR

20th Fighter Group

Herbert flew with the Eagle Squadrons, formerly composed of American volunteers in the Royal Air Force.

RICHARD "DICK" HEWITT

Dick Hewitt was born in December 1920 as one of six sons of a western New York farmer. He enlisted in the US Army Air Corps in 1941, shortly after the attack on Pearl Harbor.

78th Fighter Group

Hewitt graduated from cadet flight school and was part of one of the first replacement pilot groups to travel overseas in P-47 aircraft. He completed two tours of combat in the P-47 before completing 144 hours in the P-51 Mustang in December 1944.

Hewitt finished World War II with 425 hours in 140 combat missions, all with the 78th Fighter Group. He retired from the Air Force Reserve in 1963 with over 20 years of service.

In civilian life, Hewitt retired from the DuPont Company in 1982, after more than 29 years with the firm. He also authored a self-published book, *Target of Opportunity*, which was released with global distribution in December 2000.

Hewitt was a fighter pilot and commander of the 82nd Fighter Squadron in the 78th Fighter Group, a part of the 8th Air Force.

ROBERT A. "BOB" HOOVER

52nd Fighter Group

At 21 Bob Hoover was assigned to the 52nd Fighter Group in Sicily, one of two Spitfire groups in the Army Air Force. He flew 58 successful missions and on the 59th was shot down off the southern coast of France. He spent 16 months in Stalag Luft #1.

For his contributions, Hoover was awarded the Distinguished Flying Cross, the Soldier's Medal, the Air Medal, and the Purple Heart.

After the war, Hoover accepted a position with General Motors as a test pilot, and in 1950, he was hired by North American Aviation to do experimental flight testing on all models of the F-86 Saberjet and the Navy FJ-2 as well as the F-100.

Hoover has also set a number of world records, including a coast-to-coast flight from Los Angeles, California to Daytona Beach, Florida in a P-51. Time enroute, five hours and 20 minutes. His yellow Mustang was one of the main attractions at the Reno Air Races for many years. He also flew hundreds of airshow performances in a Shrike Commander, motivating many wide-eyed children to become pilots.

"The Mustang has been part of my life from the first moment I flew one back in the war. It is a true icon in history. When Lee Lauderback decided to have the event, I thought it was marvelous to bring so many aircraft and people together. It was really like WWII at this event with so many professionals and heroes honored. It was fantastic and a very high honor to be one of the many chosen to represent the Mustang's legacy."

ARTHUR JEFFREY

In a combat report, Arthur Jeffrey describes this particular incident:

"I was leading Newcross Yellow Section on an escort mission to Leipzig…As we approached the target area at 30,000 feet, Col. Zemke, group leader, called in enemy aircraft (E/A) were approaching the bombers in a gaggle from the North…I picked the nearest ME-109, split-'S'd down after him, and closed in on him from the rear at about 24,000 feet. Evidently sighting me, the German pulled into a sharp right turn, enabling me to get within range and fire a deflection shot. I observed many strikes on the fuselage from the cockpit to the engine. Apparently, his engine quit and the pilot must have been also been hit, for the E/A eased down into a gentle glide and I did not see the pilot make any attempt to bail out…I opened fire again getting good strikes…part of the wing flew off, and flame poured from out of the engine. The enemy aircraft then rolled gently over on its back and dived into a cloud bank."

In total, Jeffrey would claim 14 kills and three damaged, as well as being the first Allied Pilot to shoot down an ME-163, Germany's small rocket-powered interceptor.

Colonel Arthur Jeffrey earned 14 kills and three damaged, as well as being the first Allied Pilot to shoot down an ME-163, Germany's small rocket-powered interceptor.

479th Fighter Group

LEEDOM "KIRK" JOHN

John was assigned to the 55th Fighter Group where he met his first Mustang and on December 15th flew his first combat mission into Germany.

On his fourth mission after strafing a troop train and station, John and a few other squadron members closed in on some FW-190s. After many skilled maneuvers, John and his squadron destroyed five in the encounter.

On combat mission 10, John fired at an ME-109, hitting the wing roots, causing the aircraft to explode in front of him. The low level explosion flipped him on his side and nearly caused him to catch a wingtip on the ground. He landed the crippled airplane in the snow, and a man with a covered wagon led him to Brussels, away from approaching Germans.

John experienced many other close calls throughout the war and believes he survived each because, "The Lord was with him." As a member of the 55th Fighter Group, he was a member of "the first Fighter Group over Berlin, the German capital." He also learned his Mustang could travel up to 660 mph after chasing down an ME-262.

55th Fighter Group

"My wife, daughter, and grandson all got to sit in the cockpit of a Mustang where I had sat to fly over 600 hours of combat."

"I flew as *Krazy Kid* until I got shot down. Then I got a new Mustang and named it *Ornery*. Another pilot flew that one and was shot down and killed, so they gave me another plane and I named it *Ornery II, Teacher's Pet.*"

LEO HOWARD KERNS

20th Fighter Group

Leo Howard Kerns was born on June 23, 1924 in Plano, Illinois. He was one of six children, with three brothers and two sisters.

Kerns went to high school in Illinois and received his BSBA from Georgetown University School of Foreign Service in 1947, continuing on to receive a LLB/Juris Doctor degree from Georgetown Law School in 1950.

He entered the military as a Cadet in 1943, receiving his wings and commission in Jackson, Mississippi in January of 1944. Making Flight Commander by the age of 20, Kerns flew numerous combat missions using the P-51, escorting bombers and conducting strafing missions. He also performed a number of air-sea rescue missions and photo-recon missions out of King's Cliffe, England.

Kerns is credited with two German aircraft destroyed and was decorated, receiving the Distinguished Flying Cross twice and the Air Medal seven times. He mustered out of the service in November 1945.

Kerns went back to the United States, where he practiced law in Illinois and the District of Columbia.

Kerns shot down two German aircraft and received the Distinguished Flying Cross twice and the Air Medal seven times.

"I was very confident and comfortable with the Mustang. There was never any hesitation; I never had fear the way some guys had it — none of that. I just thought, 'Gee, I have a job to do. Here they are. I'm going to down as many as I can.'"

Known as "Big John" due to his broad, six-foot plus frame, an unusual size for a fighter pilot, Kirla flew a Mustang named *Spook*. The name materialized because Big John wore soft-soled shoes and, despite his size, could sneak up on anything, including the Germans. Kirla flew *Spook* with such force that he earned the distinction of being the first combat pilot to have a G-meter installed in his plane. As described by Kirla, "Occasionally we ran into fighters, and I had the problem of bending the wings of my airplane in turns. I pulled a 10.5G and bent my wings four times." After this, the G-meter was installed.

Kirla still maintains his private pilot's license and flies a Cessna from his home in Chester, Connecticut.

357th Fighter Group

On a cold February day in 1945, Andrew C. Lacy was part of a mission comprised of 48 P-51 fighters escorting an assigned box of B-17 and B-24 bombers through flak-infested skies to the Nuremberg, Germany target area. While searching for targets in the countryside, Lacy spotted a train hidden on the tracks in a heavily wooded area. Realizing it was a freight train and not a passenger train, Lacy decided to attack. After dropping his external fuel tanks he suddenly felt something slam into the underside of his aircraft. Almost immediately his cockpit filled with smoke. He was also leaking gas and smoke in large quantities…he had no choice but to bail out and was captured by German soldier.

Lacy's flying career would go on to span more than three decades. He flew over 25 military and civilian aircraft and logged over 6,500 hours of flying time, mostly in fighters. Colonel Lacy flew 50 combat missions over Europe and also served in Vietnam.

> "Seeing all of those beautiful P-51s lined up, wing tip to wing tip on the tarmac, three lines deep, will remain indelibly etched into my mind's eye forever."

4th Fighter Group

Andrew Lacy took off for combat missions out of Debden, England until his P-51 was shot down by enemy anti-aircraft fire on February 21, 1945.

As a child, Don Lopez would ride his bike to nearby airports just to watch the airplanes. Not surprisingly he joined the Army Air Force's Aviation Cadet Program as soon as the age limit was lowered to 18.

After earning his wings, he was assigned to the 23rd Fighter Group flying the P-40 Warhawk in China, the successor squadron to the famous American Volunteer Group's "Flying Tigers." Lopez claimed four aerial victories in the P-40 fighting the Japanese in China. His first confirmed kill was one of his most memorable. He had engaged in an aerial game of chicken and made a head-on pass at a Japanese KI-43 Oscar fighter, counting on the Japanese fighter "flinching first" and turning away. The opposing pilot did flinch, but by the time he began to turn it was too late and the two aircraft collided. Fortunately for Lopez, the Oscar burst into flames while his rugged P-40 lost part of a wing but safely made it back for landing. His fifth and final victory, securing his ace status, was after the squadron had transitioned to the P-51 Mustang.

23rd Fighter Group

Don Lopez flew for the first time at the age of seven in an open cockpit biplane. As a pilot, he shot down five Japanese planes, making him an ace.

PAUL McCORMICK

1937 was a memorable year for young Paul McCormick. In October, he married his high school sweetheart, Emma Price. He also started working for North American Aviation, the company that built the P-51. He was eventually promoted to Assistant Superintendent during the peak of the Mustang assemblies. He managed five departments with over 2,500 associates.

In 1951, Mr. McCormick and family moved to Columbus, Ohio where he was offered the position of Superintendent of Sheet Metal at the Columbus plant. Here, he helped transition the plant from Curtiss-Wright and increased the number of employees from 1,500 to 20,000 in two years.

Mr. McCormick "retired" in 1988 at 70 years of age but continued to serve as a consultant to North American Aviation until he finally truly retired in 1999.

In 1937, McCormick went to work for North American Aviation. He remained with the company until retirement in 1999.

"The Gathering was the crowning event of my aviation career."

CHARLES McGEE

Charles McGee earned his silver wings as a single-engine fighter pilot and was commissioned a Second Lieutenant in June 1943, graduating in class 43-F at Tuskegee Army Airfield, Alabama.

McGee remained on active duty for more than 30 years and became a command pilot with more than 6,300 total hours. He holds an Air Force record for fighter combat flying in World War II, Korea, and Vietnam, including 136 missions in P-39/P-47/P-51 aircraft with the 302nd Fighter Squadron in Italy, 100 missions in F-51 aircraft with the 67th Fighter Bomber Squadron in Korea, and 172 missions in RF-4C with the 16th Tactical Reconnaissance Squadron in Vietnam.

His awards include the Legion of Merit with Oak Leaf Cluster, the Distinguished Flying Cross with two Oak Leaf Clusters, the Bronze Star, the Air Medal with 25 Oak Leaf Clusters, the Army Commendation Medal, the Air Force Commendation Medal with Oak Leaf Cluster, the Presidential Unit Citation, the Korean Presidential Unit Citation, the Hellenic Republic World War II Commemorative Medal, the French Legend of Honor, and several campaign and service ribbons.

332nd Fighter Group

"It was great having so many young people attend and to realize that we can keep them motivated to take their place in our country's future."

Charles McGee holds an Air Force record of 409 fighter combat missions flown in World War II, Korea, and Vietnam.

Photo: Courtesy Mike Ullery for the National Aviation Hall of Fame (NAHF)

MERLE C. OLMSTEAD

After graduating from high school in 1940, the events at Pearl Harbor decided Olmstead's future, and he enlisted in the Air Corps. Less then perfect eyesight precluded him from aircrew training, and those who had to try to fit "round pegs into round holes" often decided being an aircraft mechanic was a great alternative.

After mechanics school at Sheppard Field in Texas, and a brief course on P-38s at the factory school in California, Olmstead was assigned to the newly formed 357th Fighter Group at Hamilton Field, California. This was the beginning of a life-long association with the 357th, its people, and the wonderful flying machine, the P-51 Mustang. At war's end, he went back to civilian life but soon returned to the USAF, where he remained until retirement in 1965. Another 20 years as a civilian with the USAF and U.S. Army aviation completed almost 40 years in military aviation.

Having written three books on the history of the 357th Fighter Group, Olmstead published his most recent book in 2004 titled *To War With The Oxford Boys*.

Merle Olmstead trained on P-39s in the U.S., then joined the 357th based at Boxted, Essex as part of the 9th Air Force which was blessed with P-51s from the outset.

357th Fighter Group

In the spring of 1944, Bill Overstreet of the 357th Fighter Group stayed hot on the tail of a German ME-109. The German pilot flew over Paris hoping the heavy German anti-aircraft artillery would solve his problem and eliminate Overstreet and his P-51C, the *Berlin Express*. Hoping did no good. The German's engine was hit, and Overstreet persisted through the intense enemy flak. As a last resort, the ME-109 pilot aimed his aircraft at the Eiffel Tower and in a breathtaking maneuver flew beneath it. The unshakeable Overstreet followed and scored several more hits in the process. The German plane crashed and Bill escaped the heavy flak around Paris by flying low and full throttle over the river.

Overstreet recalls the event, "I had followed this 109 from the bombers when most of the German fighters left. We had a running dogfight and I got some hits about 1,500 feet. He then led me over Paris where many guns were aimed at me. As soon as he was disabled, I ducked down just over the river and followed the river until I was away from Paris."

357th Fighter Group

Overstreet is said to have chased German fighters so close to the ground he had grass in his wingtips and barbed wire hanging from his tail.

CHARLES "BUCK" PATTILLO

In November of 1942, Buck Pattillo enlisted in the Army Air Corps as an aviation cadet. Following intensive training at various military bases, he received his wings and commission in March of 1944. He next trained in P-40 Warhawks and deployed to the European Theater of Operations where he flew combat missions with the 352nd Fighter Group. While with the 352nd he earned the Distinguished Flying Cross and Air Medal with two Oak Leaf Clusters.

In August 1952, Pattillo was assigned to the Air Training Command's 3600th Combat Crew Training Group at Luke AFB, Arizona. In 1953, he assisted in organizing the USAF Thunderbirds and flew as left wing for the original team. In February of 1954, he returned to the 3600th CCTG to become the Squadron Operations Officer, Squadron Commander, and then Group Operations Officer.

He went on to fly 120 combat missions as an F-4 Phantom pilot before ending his tour in Vietnam and eventually retiring as a Lieutenant General in the United States Air Force.

8th Air Force

"I was most impressed with the largest number of P-51 Mustangs assembled at one location since WWII. In addition, to witness so many flying in a mass formation — wow! What a show! It brought back many fond memories."

C. A. "BILL" PATTILLO

C. A. "Bill" Pattillo received his pilot's wings and commission as a Second Lieutenant in March 1944.

During World War II, Pattillo flew 135 combat missions with the 352nd Fighter Group before being shot down and captured by the Germans. He received the Distinguished Flying Cross and the Air Medal with two Oak Leaf Clusters.

In 1952, he became a fighter gunnery instructor with the 3542nd Flying Training Squadron at Pinecastle AFB in Florida. In 1953, he joined his twin brother Buck Pattillo at Luke AFB in Arizona, where they were both gunnery instructors and were instrumental in forming the first official aerial demonstration team for the U.S. Air Force, the Thunderbirds. Bill flew right wing on the original team in 1953.

Pattillo was transferred to Vietnam in 1968, where he flew 236 combat missions and was awarded the Silver Star, the Distinguished Flying Cross, the Legion of Merit, and the Air Medal with 11 Oak Leaf Clusters. Bill Pattillo retired as a Major General in 1980 after 35 years of distinguished service.

8th Air Force

Bill Pattillo is famous for shooting down a German ME-262. He was later shot down on his 135th mission and spent the rest of the war as a POW.

"In my opinion The Gathering of Mustangs and Legends was the safest, best organized and conducted airshow operation I have ever attended. The number of operational Mustangs flying, the number of aviation enthusiasts, and the old friends attending made this gathering an event of a lifetime."

William Perry was sworn into the Army Air Corps at Fort Leavenworth, Kansas and attended aviation training at Glendale, Arizona and Bakersfield, California.

Perry was assigned to the 8th Air Force, 339th Fighter Group, 503rd Fighter Squadron in Fowlmere, England. He flew 61 missions with 300 hours of combat time.

During the Korean War, Perry was assigned to the 20th Air Force in Okinawa as a Communication Staff Officer and flew the C-47 from Okinawa to Seoul.

In Vietnam, Perry flew the C-47 Gooney Bird, dropping leaflets during the day and millions of candle flares at night to provide light for the fighter attacks.

After returning to the U.S., Perry was assigned to Richard Gebrur AFB, Missouri, where he was a Staff Officer for the 10th Air Force Headquarters.

William Perry retired from military duty after 28 years of service and a total of more than six years of overseas service.

339th Fighter Group

Perry told his story in his book
Our Pilots in the Air.

JOE PETERBURS

At 19, Joseph Peterburs was assigned to the 20th Fighter Group, 55th Squadron serving in England where the group was flying the P-51 Mustang. He flew 49 missions.

On his last sortie, Peterburs chased and attacked a ME-262, slicing through the bomber formation. After injuring the German jet, Peterburs strafed an airfield several times, destroying five enemy aircraft and damaging several hangars. His Mustang took numerous hits and Peterburs had to bail out near Burg, Germany. He was immediately captured by the Germans, but Peterburs escaped and joined the Russians in the battle of Wittenburg on the river Elbe.

Colonel Peterburs retired after 36 years of military service in 1979 as a command pilot with over 2,000 hours of conventional and 2,000 hours of jet time. He flew 125 combat missions.

His decorations include: the Legion of Merit, the Distinguished Flying Cross with one Oak Leaf Cluster, the Bronze Star with one Oak Leaf Cluster, the Purple Heart with one Oak Leaf Cluster, the Air Medal with seven Oak Leaf Clusters, the POW Medal, and 32 other medals and decorations.

VICTORY BY VALOR
20th Fighter Group

"Probably the most enjoyable observation for me was seeing the eagerness and enthusiasm for the event by the younger generations, including the children. Their desire to hear the stories, smell the environment, and hear the sounds of that fantastic machine — the Mustang — was inspiring."

At 19, Peterburs was flying the P-51 Mustang with the 20th Fighter Group, 55th Squadron serving in England. He flew 49 missions before going down behind enemy lines.

PETE PETERSON

World War II brought Pete Peterson the opportunity to learn to fly, something he could not afford on his own. When the Army Air Corps accepted him, his two years of college education was interrupted.

Peterson ended up at Duxford, England, home of the 78th Fighter Group, assigned to the 83rd Fighter Squadron. On his first flight three of the 16 planes that started in horrendous weather conditions had to belly in due to the 50 to 100-foot ceiling, low fuel, and loss of sight of the air strip. Peterson was one of those three. Quite the introduction!

In January of 1945, the 78th converted to the Mustang, of which Peterson got two whole hours of practice in before heading out on a mission. Many of Peterson's missions were escort missions, but, he experienced plenty of flak. He relates, "It was a very emotional feeling to see the bombers fly into that — after the IP and on the bomb run, they could not divert and were helpless targets. I watched many a bomber go down — something I shall never forget."

"Although I have not flown as a pilot for some years, I still get a tingle in my spine when I see those Mustangs fly."

Peterson had to land his damaged P-51 in Poland. He was listed as MIA for the next six weeks until he could hitch a ride back to his unit in a B-17 bomber.

ABOVE THE FOE

78th Fighter Group

ROBERT "PUNCHY" POWELL

8th Air Force

Robert Powell entered the U.S. Army Air Corps in January 1942 and was called to active duty as an Aviation Cadet two months later. He received his primary flight training at Oxnard, California in the PT-13B Stearman aircraft.

Powell was commissioned as a 2nd Lieutenant Pilot Officer on January 4, 1943. He was transferred to England in April and assigned to RTU at Atham, U.K. April to August 1943 for additional training in P-47s.

Powell was then assigned to the 352nd Fighter Group at Bodney, East Anglia, U.K. in August 1943 and flew 87 combat missions with the 328th Squadron, 352nd Fighter Group including two combat tours and 306 combat hours. Powell was credited with six enemy aircraft destroyed, two probables, and seven damaged (air and ground) in support of ground forces before and after D-Day. He flew two D-Day missions over Normandy.

Powell's many military awards include the Air Medal with three Oak Leaf Clusters, the Distinguished Flying Cross with two Oak Leaf Clusters, the Presidential Unit Citation, the ETO Medal with four Battle Stars, the French D-Day Medal, the Victory Medal, and several campaign medals.

"Although we don't think of ourselves as heroes, The Gathering made us all feel like we were. It brought back memories of the days of our youth when we were blessed with the opportunity to fly and fight for our country in the best fighter of our time. What more could we ever ask for in our lifetime?"

The nickname for the Blue Nose P-51s, the "Blue Nosed Bastards of Bodney," is said to have come from Hermann Goering, supreme commander of Hitler's Luftwaffe. Powell flew the blue Mustangs with the 352nd Fighter Group from Bodney, England.

ALDEN RIGBY

Rigby earned his wings in December 1943 at Spence Field, Georgia and was assigned to P-51 training at Bartow, Florida in February 1944.

After briefly staying on as an instructor, Rigby requested and received an assignment to the 352nd Fighter Group at Bodney, England. His duties included dive-bombing, strafing, and escort. In December 1944, Rigby moved with the 352nd to Y-29, Asch, Belgium to help stop the Battle of the Bulge.

In January 1945, Rigby found himself directly involved with the German Operation Bodenplatte. The German operation included some 900 German aircraft assigned to hit 16 Allied airfields simultaneously. Rigby was the first plane in the air. Of the four enemy planes destroyed by Rigby that day, three were shot down after his gun sight failed.

After the battle, Rigby mistakenly claimed only 1/2 kills on two of the downed planes. And it wasn't until September 2000 that the American Fighter Aces Association, using only 8th Air Force official documentation, awarded full kills to Rigby — as did the 352nd Fighter Group in 2001, making him their 29th ace.

"I have told my family and many others that if I never see another airshow — Columbus was the ultimate — I can now be content."

8th Air Force

Alden Rigby flew 76 combat missions for a total of 272 hours in combat. He was decorated with the Silver Star, the Air Medal with seven Oak Leaf Clusters, and the Distinguished Unit Citation.

Hank Snow attended preflight, primary, basic, and advanced flying training with Class 43-I in 1943 and received his commission as a Second Lieutenant and Pilot's Wings on October 1, 1943.

His combat experience includes 100 Tactical Fighter Missions — China, Burma, and India (1944-1945); 101 Tactical Fighter Missions — Korea (1952); 335 Air Liaison/Forward Air Controller Missions — Vietnam (1965-1966); 130 Tactical Fighter Missions — Thailand (1969-1970); and one combat Parachute jump — Vietnam (1966) in the 1,000 Man Assault with Army of Vietnam (ARVN) Forces 50 miles north of Saigon in War Zone C.

Snow's honors and decorations include the Legion of Merit, the Distinguished Flying Cross (awarded six times), the Bronze Star, the Air Medal (awarded 24 times), the Air Commendation Medal, the Vietnam Cross of Gallantry with Silver Star, the Vietnam Medal of Honor, the Vietnam Staff Service Medal, the Presidential Unit Citation 2, the Air Force Outstanding Unit Award — Combat Readiness Medal.

His flying experience includes 14,000 hours total time with 2,200 hours as an instructor pilot, 125 hours instruments (845 actual weather), 1,400 hours at night, and 1,602 hours in combat.

8th Air Force

Snow flew 100 Tactical Fighter Missions – China, Burma, and India (1944-1945); 101 Tactical Fighter Missions – Korea (1952), and 130 Tactical Fighter Missions – Thailand (1969-1970).

"It was a wonderful tribute to all our military pilots, mechanics, etc. who were in World War II in primitive conditions and being 21 years old and flying the P-51."

FRANK E. SPEER

4th Fighter Group

While flying a P-51 Mustang near Poland, Speer was shot down and walked nearly 400 miles across northern Germany in an attempt to reach Denmark. He was captured after collapsing from exhaustion and lack of food.

Speer served 11 months in three different Stalags and was forced to participate in the grueling "Death March" to Nuremberg. His third escape attempt was successful and, with help from a group of French forced laborers, Speer and a friend captured 24 German soldiers and an officer.

During his career, Speer was awarded The Distinguished Flying Cross, The Air Medal with three Oak Leaf Clusters, and the Presidential Unit Citation. He was discharged in 1946, but continued to serve in the Air Force Reserve until 1955.

Speer is the author of three books about the 4th Fighter Group in World War II, titled *Wingman*, *The Debden Warbirds*, and *One Down, One Dead*. He is active in veterans' organizations and in speaking to non-profit groups such as schools, libraries, and civic organizations.

On his 17th mission, Speer was shot down and became a prisoner of war. He and a companion escaped and made their way back to Allied Forces on May 29, 1945.

HARRY STEWART, JR.

Harry Stewart completed flight training at Tuskegee Air Field in Alabama and was awarded his wings and commissioned as a 2nd Lieutenant while still a teenager.

He was sent to Italy to serve in the 332nd Fighter Group. He flew 43 bomber escort missions with the 15th Air Force and was credited with destroying three enemy aircraft in aerial combat. He was awarded the Distinguished Flying Cross as well as the Air Medal with six Oak Leaf Clusters.

After returning to the U.S., Stewart further distinguished himself as a member of the wining team in the 1949 USAF Gunnery Meet held at Nellis AFB, Nevada.

After being discharged in 1950, Stewart returned to his hometown and attended New York University, where he earned a bachelor's degree in mechanical engineering. He retired as a Lieutenant Colonel.

In his civilian life, Stewart retired as Vice President of ANR Pipeline Company, a major interstate natural gas consortium. Stewart still enjoys flying and frequently flies neighborhood kids around in his Schweizer motorglider.

332nd Fighter Group

As a member of the all-black 332nd Fighter Group, Stewart flew 43 combat missions in the P-51 Mustang. He left the Air Force with the rank of Lieutenant Colonel.

DONALD J. STRAIT

During his tour with the 356th Fighter Group, Donald Strait participated in long range bomber escort missions as well as air-to-ground support. In November of 1944, Strait began flying P-51 Mustangs.

On one mission Strait led 16 P-51s into battle against 40 German BF-109s. A few moments later, he counted over 100 more German fighters preparing to attack the American bombers. After a considerable amount of dogfighting, fuel ran low and the fighters had to return to base. Strait's squadron recorded 23 German fighter kills that day without losing a single Mustang.

By the end of the war, Donald Strait had completed two combat tours, 122 missions in the P-47 and P-51, and racked up 13.5 enemy aircraft kills. He received the Silver Star, Legion of Merit, Distinguished Flying Cross with two Oak Leaf Clusters, Air Medal with 14 Oak Leaf Clusters, Presidential Unit Citation, Victory Medal, European Theater Ribbon with four Battle Stars, American Defense Ribbon, USAF Exceptional Civilian Service Award, and Republic of Vietnam Gallantry Cross with Palm (1966-1970). Don retired from the United States Air Force in 1978 with the rank of Major General.

"The Gathering of Mustangs and Legends meant very much to me as it represented an opportunity to renew friendships with many fighter pilots whom I served with during my 38 years in the Air Force...

The opening ceremony presented the American flag and national anthem in the most dramatic manner I have ever witnessed."

8th Air Force

In 1944 Strait began flying P-51 Mustangs as the commander of the 361st Fighter Squadron during his second combat tour.

Following graduation from high school, Reg Urschler enlisted in the U.S. Air Force and completed Basic Training at Sampson AFB, Geneva, New York. Next he became an aviation cadet, completing primary flight training at Hondo AB, Texas and basic flight training at Vance AFB, Enid, Oklahoma. He was commissioned a Second Lieutenant and received his pilot wings in August 1955.

Urschler's military career included numerous tours of duty in Japan, Turkey, Greenland, England, and Alaska.

Urschler is a command pilot with more than 15,000 flying hours, over 1,500 of which were in combat, and over 3,000 in the P-51 Mustang. His military decorations include the Distinguished Service Medal, Legion of Merit, Distinguished Flying Cross, Bronze Star, Meritorious Service Medal, Air Medal with 18 Oak Leaf Clusters, and Air Force Commendation Medal with three Oak Leaf Clusters. He retired with the rank of Brigadier General.

Brigadier General Urschler is an honorary member of the Tuskegee Airmen.

> "It was a helluva historical aviation event, probably never to be repeated again. Those who attended were indeed fortunate to have had the opportunity to view this vast array of World War II P-51 Mustangs...and those who flew them."

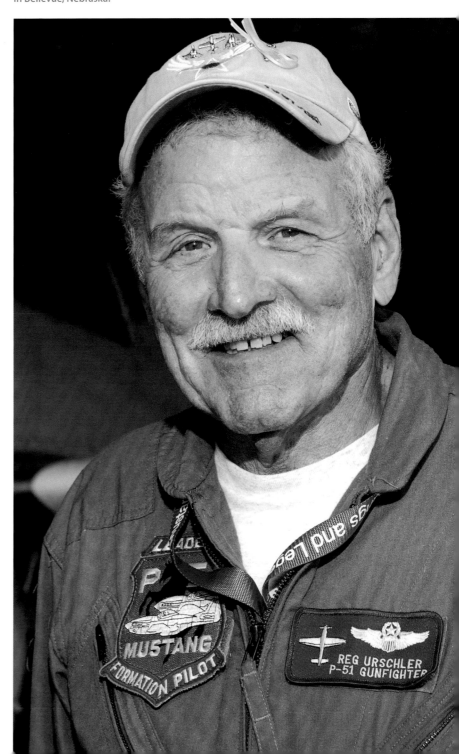

Reg Urschler flew GunFighter, a P-51 with the Commemorative Air Force, for 30 years. He estimates he's logged more than 3,300 hours over 1,950 flights. He retired as a Brigadier General and lives in Bellevue, Nebraska.

ERNIE WAKEHOUSE

Wakehouse flew 100 missions in P-51s, but on a particular flight November 18, 1951, he distinguished himself by extraordinary achievement.

He led his flight of Mustangs in a series of devastating attacks, using napalm, rockets, and machine guns on enemy troops, troop bunkers, and supplies near Songdong-ni, Korea. Despite the poor visibility and opposition, Wakehouse pressed the attacks onward and left the area only after all ordinances had been expended. Lt. Wakehouse returned his flight home safely.

Those attacks resulted in 40 enemy troops killed personally by Wakehouse, 60 others by the remainder of the flight, and numerous destroyed enemy bunkers, thus hampering the enemy's operations in the area. Wakehouse was given the Award of the Distinguished Flying Cross for his courageous efforts.

Later Wakehouse went on a pre-briefed mission to an enemy supply and bivouac area near Pyongang, North Korea. This flight, "accounted for the destruction of four enemy vehicles, three large secondary explosions, and the destruction of the entire supply and bivouac area." Every member of the flight was recommended for award for their persistence in the face of intense enemy fire.

Ernie Wakehouse joined the Army Air Corp in 1942 and received his wings in December of 1944. He flew P-40s and P-51s in World War II and the Korean War.

"I have attended a lot of airshows during my 86 years and yours was the very best."

Charles E. "Charlie" Wilson was involved in what is believed to be the first successful rescue of a downed flyer behind enemy lines by a second aircraft during World War II.

After 20 minutes of strafing a rail marshalling yard, the Mustangs were low on both ammo and fuel. Just as they were about to head for home, one of them spotted a moving train and requested permission to attack. One pass was approved. Wilson sprayed the cab area with his last 200 rounds of .50 caliber armor–piercing incendiary bullets and the whole locomotive blew up just as he arrived overhead. The flying debris took out his coolant system and the aircraft started down.

A few moments later Major Wyatt Exum landed nearby. After a running gun battle between Wilson and the Germans, Exum got his airplane back in the air.

Exum was awarded a Silver Star for his heroism. Wilson and Exum stayed in touch until Exum's death. According to Wilson, "If it weren't for Wyatt Exum, I probably wouldn't be here, nor would my six children and grandchildren. I am forever indebted to him for that."

52nd Fighter Group

Major Wyatt Exum landed his P-51 behind enemy lines to rescue downed fellow pilot, Charles E. Wilson. The ploy was successful, though his aircraft suffered some bullet holes on the climb out.

JACK ZIANNI

479th Fighter Group

"About six months after becoming operational, we got the P-51 Mustang, and what a joy it was to work on this magnificent airplane," Jack Zianni said. "The P-38 was a wonderful airplane but difficult to maintain, unlike the P-51 which was a mechanic's dream. I got a thrill every time a Mustang took off…"

Zianni was a member of a group having the distinction of getting a German fighter the first day of operations and downing the last German fighter on the last day of the war. Though an aircraft mechanic throughout the war, Zianni did get the chance to fly. For fun, his squadron modified a P-38 to accommodate the enlisted and other non-flying personnel. Zianni states, "One of the best memories was zooming straight up through the solid overcast clouds of a typical English day and bursting through into the brilliant sunlight with a layer of cotton below the stretching horizon."

Zianni enlisted in the Army Air Force and served as an assistant crew chief for the P-51 Mustangs based at Wattisham Air Force Base in England.

"Incredible as it may seem, any time I see a picture of a P-51, I still get excited all over!"

DAVID LEE "TEX" HILL

After college graduation in 1938, David Lee "Tex" Hill traveled to Florida for Naval Flight Training. He was commissioned a Naval Ensign in 1939 and ordered to report to the USS Saratoga and serve in a torpedo squadron. On the Saratoga, Hill flew the Douglass TBD-1. When a General called for volunteers to form his American Volunteer Group (AVG), a group that would come to be known as the "Flying Tigers," Hill was one of the first in line.

23rd Fighter Group

During his time with the "Flying Tigers," Hill became a triple ace, destroying more than 18 enemy aircraft, including the first Japanese Zero shot down by a P-51 Mustang.

Chased from one location to another by Japanese air and ground forces, the "Flying Tigers" took to the skies time and again to defeat Japanese aircraft. Hill and his fellow pilots got their fuel, ammunition, and supplies whenever they could, performed aircraft maintenance under trees, and lived in small enclaves under constant enemy attack.

Despite these conditions, during an eight-month period, the "Flying Tigers" downed 297 Japanese aircraft — 12 of which were shot down by Hill.

Hill was a World War II triple ace, credited with being the first P-51 pilot to shoot down a Japanese Zero.

VI COWDEN

Vi Cowden spent her childhood and adolescence on a South Dakota farm where she would watch hawks fly high and moments later zoom down to capture a chicken. As she says, "that's when, as a seven-year-old child, my dream to fly like a hawk began."

WASP
Women Air Force Service Pilots

At the urging of Jacqueline Cochran, Cowden joined the Navy's WASPs. Vi Cowden was then chosen to attend Pursuit School in Brownsville, Texas. She had ten hours in the back of an AT-6 with an instructor that had never flown with a woman. He dominated the controls. When he was about to wash her out, telling her she had given him the lousiest landing he had ever experienced, she retorted, "That was not my landing. It was yours." He let her fly after that.

Vi Cowden went on to fly the North American P-51. One of her orders included delivering a Mustang to Montgomery, Alabama and upon landing she found the press was there to take pictures of her and the plane. This was all because she was the first woman to fly a P-51 to the Tuskegee Airmen.

Vi Cowden was one of 25,000 women who applied for the WASP training program. Only 1,830 were accepted and 1,074 graduated.

GATHERING FOUNDATION

Mission Statement

The mission of The Gathering Foundation, Inc. is to assist in preserving the legacy of the remaining vintage fighter aircraft throughout the world by sustaining their history and contribution to aviation.

The interest in historical aviation runs far and wide and spans many generations, from those who flew and maintained aircraft during their service years, to those who work diligently to preserve the glorious history of combat aircraft through restoration. The Gathering Foundation works to support the collection, exchange, and archive of information as it pertains to vintage fighter aircraft and the brave men and women who flew or serviced these aircraft in war times.

Foundation Board of Directors - 2011

Major General Kenneth M. (Mike) DeCuir, USAF (Ret.)
President and Director

Angela West
Vice President and Executive Director

Major General David Robinson, USAF (Ret.)
Vice President and Director

Pete Tattersall
Treasurer and Director

John Lauderback
Director

Arthur R. Louv
Director

Don Nixon
Director

Angela West
GML Event Director; V.P. & Executive Director of The Gathering Foundation

Angela's vision for The Gathering of Mustangs and Legends and her leadership of The Gathering Foundation stems from a deep passion for aviation history and honoring the memory of those who contributed so selflessly to preserving our freedom. An accomplished pilot herself, Angela's vision for the event never waivered and without her dedication, perseverance, and absolute love for aviation, The Gathering of Mustangs and Legends and The Gathering Foundation would not be possible.

Gathering Foundation Event Staff

Event Director
Angela West
Vice President, Stallion 51 Corp.

Director of Flight Operations
Lee C. Lauderback
President, Stallion 51 Corp.

Director of Operations
Bobbi Thompson
Executive Vice President, Airport Bus. Solutions

Air Boss
Wayne Boggs
President, Air Boss & Consulting Int'l

Ramp Boss
Jim Tucciarone
Air Boss & Consulting, Int'l

Legends Coordinator
Annette Calicoat

P-51 Mustang Coordinators
John Lauderback
Julie Clevenger

Sponsorship Coordinator
Wendy Stoneman

Housing/Hotels
Sue & Jerry Crady

Transportation
Bruce Turner

National Media
Lyn Freeman

Special Events Coordinator
Debi Casullo
Southern Hospitality

Video/Documentary
Ed Shipley
Strategic Message Solutions
Steve Purcell
SLP Productions

Columbus Regional Airport Authority Event Staff

Host Airport Chair
Rod C. Borden, A.A.E.
Senior Vice President & COO

Airport Operations & Logistics Chair
Charlie Goodwin, A.A.E.
General Manager, Rickenbacker International Airport

Airport Operations & Logistics Vice-Chair
Mark Mulchaey
General Manager, Bolton Field Airport

Public Relations, Rickenbacker 65th, & Tuskegee Recognition Chair
Angie Tabor
Communications Manager

Volunteer Chair
Linda Frankl, A.A.E.
Airport Operations Director

Field Services Chair
Rick Roberts
Manager, Airfield - LCK

Vendor/Exhibitor Chair
Paul Kennedy
Supervisor of Environmental Safety, & Health

Chalets, Tents, & Reserved Seating Chair
Bob Mauldin
Public Safety Manager

Parking & Ground Transportation Chair
Randy Bush, CIA, CPA
Director of Parking, Ground Transportation, and Audit Services

Public Safety Chair
Chief Richard Morgan
Public Safety Director

Technology Chair
Jim Bodi

Thank You, Volunteers!

The Gathering of Mustangs and Legends was abundantly supported by more than 750 volunteers. Each of these volunteers generously gave their time to help make this historic aviation event a success. The Gathering Foundation, Inc. graciously thanks each of the men, women, and service organizations that arrived early and remained late to accomplish the various tasks required, ensuring each event fan had a memorable experience.

Developing, staging, and producing an aviation event with all the complexities required of The Gathering of Mustangs and Legends could not be accomplished without the dedicated efforts of volunteers completing tasks — from towing aircraft and escorting historic figures to cooking hamburgers, collecting trash, and providing support for military guests. Several of the volunteers worked days or sometimes weeks to accomplish their assignments.

The Gathering Foundation, Inc. is forever indebted to our volunteers; we sincerely thank you and hope that your experience was all you wished it to be.

Sincerely,

Kenneth M. DeCuir
President
The Gathering Foundation, Inc.

Angela West
Vice President, Event Director
The Gathering Foundation, Inc.

The Gathering of Mustangs and Legends would not have been possible without the generous assistance of so many wonderful organizations and individuals. Together these organizations helped transform our celebration from concept to reality so that all attendees, young and old, could share and enjoy the heritage of aviation and the Legends who helped to create it.

Organizations, Contributors, & Friends

121st Air Refueling Wing
AEP
AeroShell
Airshow Buzz
Budweiser
Chase
Cirrus Design
Columbus Regional Airport Authority
Jack Cook
Creative Spot
Cummins Bridgeway
Experience Columbus
Ron Fagen
Barbara and Fred Fehsenfeld
Flying Magazine
Andy Frederick
Tom and Dan Friedken
Garth's Auctions
Jim Goodwin
Jim Hagedorn
Randy Haskin
History Preservation Associates
Mark Huffsletler
Hy-Tek
John Deere
K.T. Budde-Jones
Brad Lauderback
Lee Lauderback

Peter and Richard Lauderback
Lewis Energy Group
Ray Lonsdale
Dave Marco
Mills James
MustangsMustangs.com
National Aviation Hall of Fame
Nationwide
NBC 4
Ohio Army and Air National Guard
Ohio Magazine
Pepsi
Mark Peterson
Stan Piet
Rickenbacker International Airport
Don Schoen
Scotts Miracle-Gro
Lew Shaw
Sprint/Nextel
Stallion 51 Corporation
Jeff Thorton
United States Air Force
Warbird Depot
Warbird Digest
WCMH
Chris Woods
Wright Patterson Air Force Base

Photographers

Jessica Ambats
Andy Bershaw
Jean-Marie Brigant
Paul Bowen
Jarrod Cotter
James DeCamp
John Dibbs
Doug Fisher
Curtis Fowles
Atsushi "Fred" Fujimori
Ron Gafney
Scott Germain
Uwe Glaser
Arnold Greenwell
Jane Handley
Max Haynes
Mike Hemming

Erik Hildebrandt
David Leininger
Grady Lisk
Peter Lubig
Xavier Meal
Matt Meintel
Betty Meyer
Greg Morehead
Dan Patterson
Dick Phillips
Larry Rector
Julien Robin
Norbert Rotter
Scott Slocum
Tom Smith
Jim Wilson

MUSTANGS FOREVER

**To the Men and Women in Our Armed Forces Who Made
the Ultimate Sacrifice Defending Our Freedom**